SCULPTURE

Material and Process

Eduardo Paolozzi, *Tokio*, 1964. Welded aluminum painted.

DONALD J. IRVING

SCULPTURE
Material and Process

VNR VAN NOSTRAND REINHOLD COMPANY
NEW YORK CINCINNATI TORONTO LONDON MELBOURNE

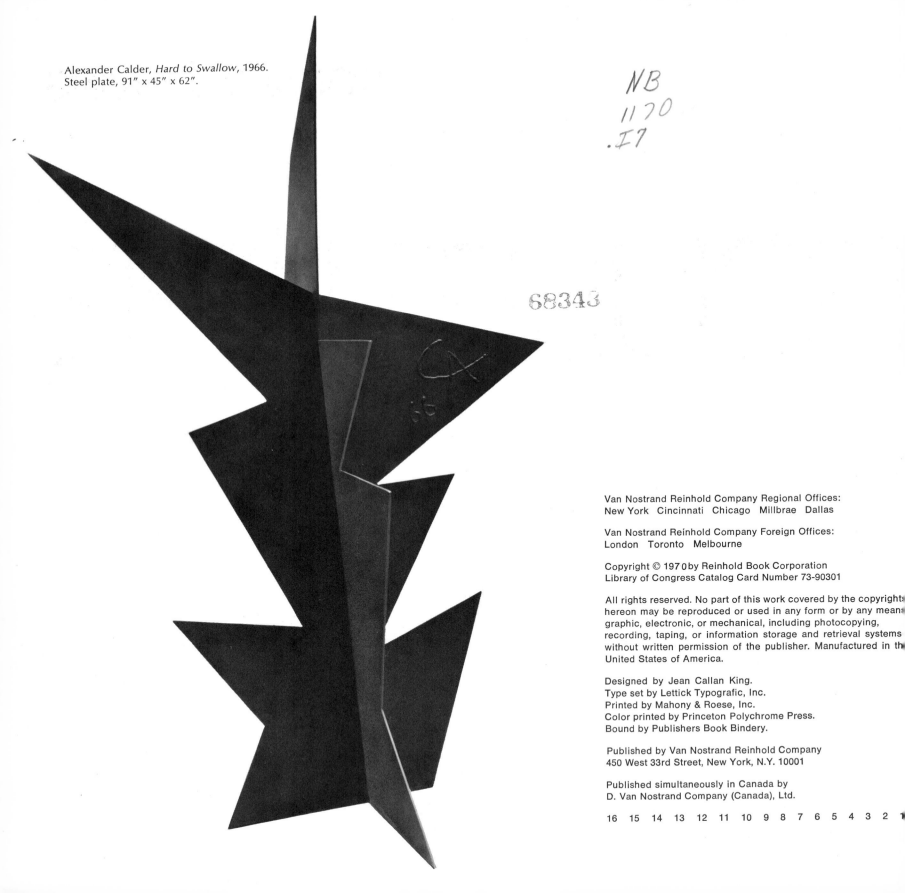

Alexander Calder, *Hard to Swallow*, 1966.
Steel plate, 91" x 45" x 62".

NB
1170
.I7

68343

Van Nostrand Reinhold Company Regional Offices:
New York Cincinnati Chicago Millbrae Dallas

Van Nostrand Reinhold Company Foreign Offices:
London Toronto Melbourne

Copyright © 1970 by Reinhold Book Corporation
Library of Congress Catalog Card Number 73-90301

Designed by Jean Callan King.
Type set by Lettick Typografic, Inc.
Printed by Mahony & Roese, Inc.
Color printed by Princeton Polychrome Press.
Bound by Publishers Book Bindery.

Published by Van Nostrand Reinhold Company
450 West 33rd Street, New York, N.Y. 10001

Published simultaneously in Canada by
D. Van Nostrand Company (Canada), Ltd.

16 15 14 13 12 11 10 9 8 7 6 5 4 3 2 1

To Jaye

ACKNOWLEDGMENTS

William Mahoney

Mildred Fairchild

Jack Mays

Michael Hall

Stanley Mock

Carol Forgione

Justin Schorr

Contents

el jet tapped from open-hearth furnace.
urtesy of United States Steel Corporation.

Chris Jeffries photo.

Introduction

Our environment abounds with provocations to sensitive visual response. Every aspect of our surroundings — the usual, often overlooked, even the mundane — holds a potential for enriching our lives and expressions in direct proportion to our ability to perceive them and share in their existence. Each of us functions simultaneously as censor, evaluator, selector, and organizer of the visual world. The prospective artist must expand and enrich his vision through development of his perceptual awareness. To create forms which transcend banal stereotypes, he must exercise his individual sensibilities, formulate unique and personal interpretations, and remain open to new experience — develop, in short, the qualities which we marvel at in children.

We are constantly confronted with things as they are, not as we wish them to be. But to see things as they are, to perceive the subtleties which distinguish each object and moment requires a process of visualizing which does away with preconceptions. We become, then, aware of relationships rather than objects and moments in isolation and we bring order and meaning to vision. The *act of seeing* in this sense is a creative one, a process of relating, arranging, and structuring visual images.

Wik photo.

Helene Patterson photo.

K. Daly photo.

Caroline Acten photo.

Joyce Pech photo.

The visual and dimensional environment through which the sculptor moves has a direct and significant impact upon his work. Sculpture is dependent upon structuring visual experience and the ancillary sensations of touch and movement. Three-dimensional experiences are directly related to physical make-up: sizes of objects are understood in terms of our dimensions; the tension of angles and balance are measured against our own equilibrium. There are no boundaries in space, only guideposts, and the sculptor who attempts to define and structure it must refine his spatial judgments and establish interpretations from his own experiences and explorations.

Chris Jeffries photo.

Machine technology, its systems and products, have altered man's world to a significant degree. Most of his time is spent in man-made environments; the contemporary landscape is largely steel and concrete. Structures developed to serve and protect man from nature are those to which he now responds, often with few or no precedents to guide him. Classical "laws of natural order" and traditions establishing a "cultural hierarchy" are an insufficient basis for judgment at a time when the total environment is undergoing change at an ever increasing rate and during a period of material abundance conceivable only in terms of assembly-line production. An inability to deal with the excesses of production is evident in the blight of urban slums not thirty years old or junk yards dotting rural roadways. Many sculptors have used the discards of industry

Jack Rivers photo.

Paula Narbutovski photo.

as the material of their art. In their assemblages of junk and mechanical parts they assign a new formal role to objects which previously had a role of utility.

The landscape is constantly being altered by man as he builds. We move in a series of patterns largely shaped by geometric configurations and structural principles. Our homes and roadways are aligned in rows and evolve as progressions of the square and rectangular module — predictable but often unfortunate amendments to a landscape cultivated, fertilized, irrigated, and deforested.

The exercise of vision and the capacity for sharing a common and brilliant vision is essential to navigate the chaos of this new environment and to draw upon available resources for the solution of form problems unique to this time.

Robert Murray, *Plainfield*, 1966. 9½′ high. Collection of Aldrich Museum, Ridgefield, Connecticut. Courtesy of Betty Parsons Gallery, New York.

Carolyn Acten photo.

Art from Technology–The New Aesthetic 2

Of major significance in the life and expressions of today is the rapidity with which technical means expand the boundaries of the contemporary world. Most of the concepts and images by which we orient ourselves to our environment are unique to this time. As methods of rapid transportation are developed, distances are reduced. Instant communication transmits information about an artist's work as soon as it is completed. The availability of such information has caused Andy Warhol to predict a time when "everyone will be famous for fifteen minutes."

But constant confrontation with mechanical and scientific devices which bombard our sensibilities is physically and emotionally exhausting. A situation of alarming proportions inevitably developed as the ideas and objects designed to meet man's emotional needs became less and less related to the devices and systems devised to meet his physical ones. Lewis Mumford in his book *Art and Technics* spoke eloquently of his concern over the dehumanizing elements of technology, comparing them with the walls of a prison.

Now those walls have been breached if not entirely destroyed by many of our contemporaries. Artists are no longer admitting technology's role of confinement as Mumford identified it but are responding to its fascination with exhilaration and invention. It is clear from much recent work that artists whose aim is still to respond to basic human needs and values are accepting not only the knowledge and tools offered by the scientific-industrial establishment but also the challenge posed by the large scale and complex elements of today's existence.

Courtesy of General Motors Corporation.

Courtesy of United States Steel Corporation.

15

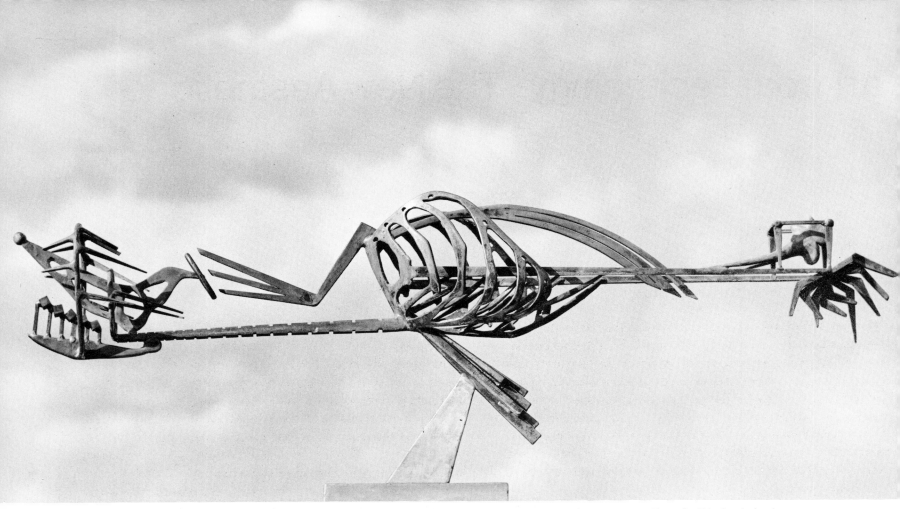

David Smith, *Royal Bird,* 1948. Stainless steel, 21³/₄" x 59". Courtesy of Walker Art Center, Minneapolis, Minnesota. Photo by Eric Sunderland.

The wide range of materials and the technical superiority essential to an industrial society have provided resources for the sculptor of today which would have been unimaginable in any other period. Ceramic-metal combinations with high thermal resistance for use in space travel, structural steel which never needs painting or protection from weather for exterior applications, and thousands of other metal alloys with an almost limitless range of qualities are some of the materials developed and perfected by industry. Industrial techniques have evolved to suit industry's needs, primarily out of a concern for efficiency of process. Mechanical duplication, standardization of product, and measured tolerance control are typical determinants of industrial techniques to which enormous resources have been committed. The resultant high degree of control over production by industry has impressed contemporary sculptors. From industry they have selected and applied certain materials and techniques to their own purposes.

A high degree of control over process permits an intimacy with materials and technique that many sculptors require. In each stage of a work they can directly control, react to, and take advantage of developments. Experimentation and spontaneity of expression are vital elements and they require a method of working and a range of material at once immediate and permanent.

Of the many materials from industry having potentialities for sculpture, metals have made the greatest impact. Techniques most often used are the direct metal welding, cutting, and brazing processes as well as studio foundry methods. The application of such processes to sculpture impose limitations and require considerations that are well known to industry. When such sculptural problems are solved, they are what David Smith called "industrialized."

To fabricate a finished piece of sculpture requires a concept in unity with the method, a recognition of the change in forces, a knowledge of the limitations and a respect for the virtues of material and method. This concept already exists in industry and to a lesser extent in architecture. Fabricated sculpture is in a certain sense 'industrialized,' in that it uses both industrial methods and materials and makes possible the rapid multiplication of a given piece. (David Smith, "Sculpture," *Architectural Record*.)

"Industrialized" in this sense, however, is not to be equated with a single way of working or with a standardized technique. Resources borrowed from industry have permitted a flexibility and control that has technically liberated the sculptor. They provide an array of techniques and materials as unique and personal as the sculptor wishes to make them.

New materials and methods developed by industry have not only increased the artist's facility for dealing with established concepts but have encouraged him to experiment widely. Media and experimentation, supporting and extending his imagery, form an integral part of the artist's personal vision. A technique can both inspire and limit form achievement; on the other hand, the artist's vision often causes him to adapt or alter the technique and creates new possibilities for its application.

To understand why a sculptor decides to work within the limitations of a traditional technique, to develop a traditional method of working for unique purposes, or to adopt new materials and processes, it is best to listen to the artist himself. The following quotations from the writings of Nickford and de Creeft show clearly the impact of materials and techniques from industry and the potential they hold for the sculptor in achieving his expressive purposes.

The possibilities offered to the sculptor by new methods and techniques for working in metals are practically unlimited. He is no longer bound to the block concept of carving nor dependent upon the foundry for the permanency of his works. He is able to concentrate all of his efforts on the actual act of creation without undue concern over the material itself. (Jaun Nickford, "New Talent U.S.A.," *Art in America*.)

Conrad Marca-Relli, *RXL-4*, 1966. Aluminum, 57" x 54" x 4". Courtesy of Marlborough-Gerson Gallery, New York. Photo by Adolph Studly.

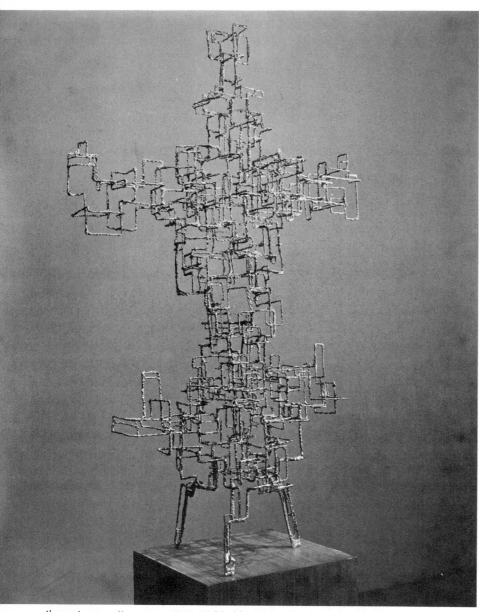

Ibram Lassaw, *Kwannon*, 1952. Welded bronze with silver, 6' high. Collection, The Museum of Modern Art, New York. Katherine Cornell Fund.

Though most of my work has been in the form of direct carving i wood or stone, I have worked and experimented with nearly all avai able materials, particularly in beaten lead, hammered copper, and t and metal construction. In 1925 for example, I used stovepipes, o cans, bicycle tubes, insulated wire, and all kinds of odds and enc and pieces of "junk" to create my *Picador*. This piece was designe to show the inflated pride of those gendarmes of the bull ring they rode their half-dead martyrized horses. This rider carried a cu tain rod lance and the gored horse spilled tubes and wire from h belly. The *Picador* caused considerable comment in Paris when it wa shown and most of the discussion centered around its validity i terms of the materials employed. But the *Picador* and his materia were one; he could not have come into existence without then (Jose de Creeft, "Statement on Sculpture," *7 Arts #2*, p. 63.)

In selecting his materials the sculptor has been faced wit economic problems more serious than those that prevail upo other contributors to the visual arts. The traditional material marble, bronze, and fine blocks of wood, are expensive, an often because of their expense the sculptor needed a commis sion before he could work. In dealing with contemporary co problems many sculptors have found that the materials an methods of industry which permit them to work less expen sively and more directly are also those which best express th period in which they live. Lassaw, Smith, and Lippold have a commented on these issues:

. . . not only is it absolutely necessary from an economic point c view that the sculptor develop new media which do not involve e> pensive casting, but it is also traditional for the artist of each age t make use of the materials and means available to him. (Ibram Lassa\ quoted in Martitia Sawin, "Ibram Lassaw," *Arts*, p. 22.)

The material called iron or steel I hold in high respect. What it ca do in arriving at a form economically, no other material can do. Th metal possesses little art history. What associations it possesses ar those of this century: power, structure, movement, progress, suspen sion, destruction, brutality. (David Smith, "The New Sculpture: Symposium.")

I like to feel that material which can be shaped at white heat and i subject to various nuances of chemical action is the best means fo implementing this spirit embodied in the work of this period. Som people feel that technology is inhuman, but machinery is part o human thought. Look into the engine of a car — how wonderful i is, what precision, what order. It seems to me that artists who rebe against their times or go to the other extremes are both equall

Lee Bontecou, *Untitled*, 1966. Mixed media, 78½" x 119" x 31".
Courtesy of Leo Castelli Gallery, New York. Photo by Rudolph Burckhardt.

Installation of David Smith show, Institute of Contemporary Art, University of Pennsylvania, 1964.

wrong. Artists are never rebels, nor can they escape into the future or into the past. Carving directly in stone — a big thing for sculptors in the 'twenties' and 'thirties' —was all right for medieval artists. For them it must have seemed a wonderful new thing. Working methods and materials should always be proper to the age in which the artist works; materials should both give to and receive from the artist's concepts. (Theodore Roszak, *Fourteen Americans*.)

Processes which allow the sculptor to work directly with the materials of the final form have great appeal to contempo-

rary sculptors. Such processes provide the means by which the sculptor can completely control his work from start to finish and release him from a dependency upon foundrymen or others for permanency. Smith has said:

In work progress, I control the entire process from start to finish. There are no in-between craftsmen, or process disortions. It is the complete and total processing of the work of art. Economically this process has high virtue over other metal means. (David Smith, "The New Sculpture: A Symposium.")

The relationship between the sculptor's concept of form, and the technical means which he employs are discussed in statements by sculptors Albert and Lassaw:

I have always found it impossible in my work to make a separation between the mechanics of art and its esthetics; the imaginative and emotional content that I wanted to express have driven me to use metal in new ways. The fact that these methods have proved useful to other artists has encouraged me to go further in my exploration. (Calvin Albert, quoted in Sam Hunter, "New York, Art Capital of the East," *Art in America*.)

The use of unfamiliar metals produces additional problems so that every new work is a step into the unknown, more than with any other kind of creation. (Some processes he compares with mystical attitudes.) The modern artist is the counterpart, in our time, of the alchemist-philosopher who once toiled over furnaces, alembics and crucibles, ostensibly to make gold, but who unconsciously entered the most profound levels of being, philosophizing over the melting and mixing of the various ingredients. (Ibram Lassaw, quoted in Lawrence Campbell, "Lassaw makes a Sculpture," *Art News*.)

John Chamberlain, *Norma Jean Rising*, 1967. Galvanized steel, 66" x 38" x 38". Courtesy of Leo Castelli Gallery, New York. Photo by Rudolph Burckhardt.

Edward Higgins, *Untitled*, 1964. Welded steel and epoxy, 22" x 10" x 13". Collection, William Zierler. Courtesy of Leo Castelli Gallery, New York. Photo by Rudolph Burckhardt.

21

Herbert Ferber, *Three Arches*, 1966. Epoxy and plexiglass. Courtesy of Andre Emmerich Gallery, New York.

As indicated in many of the preceding statements, sculptors themselves have recognized and testified to the impact on their art of "materials and techniques derived from industry." What these sculptors have said or written merely supports what is already obvious in their work. Roszak, given a 6000-degree oxy-acetylene flame, invented a direct metal technique of modeling steel. Smith relies heavily on the character of the material to achieve his forms. The many technical adaptations and industrial materials which characterize sculpture today remain, however, conveyors of concept. Today, as always, techniques and materials and craftsmanship are simply means, and as such they are subordinate to the expressive purposes of sculpture. A tendency to technical virtuosity for its own sake is an inherent danger in a time when the "craft" of sculpture is undergoing such change. The sculptors Ferber and Roszak have said:

When the new techniques are mistaken for new plastic ideas and when the materials are held in reverence; when one hears a voice pitched in awesome eulogy on high melting points, as one used to hear it extoll the virtue of carving in the hardest stone and wood, art goes out the door. Since sculptors themselves are guilty of being seduced by the fetish of the material, as if they were artisans, it is not surprising to find the business of techniques distorted into a major esthetic value and find exhibitions the motivation of which is the display of virtuosity in new materials. The value of a work simply does not depend on the materials of which it is made, and a fine work gives the impression of having sprung completely formed from the artist's hand. I do not wish to impute divinity to the artist, but simply to imply that his mastery should be such that one is aware only of his vision and not of sweat. (Herbert Ferber, "The New Sculpture: A Symposium.")

Today, a great deal of emphasis is placed upon form and content as being indigenous to a media that registers experience by direct visual response. This form of direct visual sensation is primary and valid, as far as it goes — but I patently reject it as a concept sufficiently capable of ordering the visual element on any other than a primary level. (Theodore Roszak, *Fourteen Americans.*)

In many of the comments cited above sculptors have indicated their adoption of new methods of working and the utilization of new materials in order to achieve their purposes. In their search for an expressive vocabulary indigenous to their time artists have made numerous selections from the vast resources of industry. The significance of the selections and their sculptural application are such that totally new approaches to sculptural problems have emerged.

The scientific-industrial resource is far vaster and more pervasive in its influence on sculptural developments than can be suggested in a limited discussion of techniques and materials by sculptors. It amounts to a new combine between art and technology. The progress of such a combine is well illustrated by the great variety of objects in museums and galleries which light up, move, create sound, and involve the use of sophisticated electronic components. The realms of the artist and the engineer join to establish a force of considerable impact in the visual arts of our era. Artists and technicians working together are re-establishing relationships between disciplines which have grown apart with the trend toward super-specialization. The results of such collaborative efforts have produced works of pathos, humor, joy, and humanism — elements rarely associated with modern industrial technology.

The artist's role as innovator is long established. When he now turns to modern technology not only for mechanical means but for an inspirational base, he is dispelling many fears. Scientific encroachment on the human condition seems less imminent; in fact the artist's concepts and experiences hold hope for a healthier relationship between man and his machines.

Theodore Roszak, *Sentinel*, 1968. Bronze, 23' x 27'. Sculpture on site.

Perception—Process—Product

3

Sculpture can only be realized in terms of various media and processes employed to manipulate material. Of prime importance in the education of students of sculpture are: experiences with materials, experimentation with means of treating or changing them, understandings which accrue from specific applications, and the eventual control of such materials for expressive purposes. A critical function of such education is to provide fertile ground in which the student can formulate techniques and experiences that will assist the development of his capabilities for creative expression. It is necessary that the student continually expand and enlarge his conceptual language by all means available. The means which industry has made available to the student of sculpture have changed the concept of craftsmanship and requirements for training the sculptor: Moholy-Nagy has written:

The new sculptor will become again a splendid craftsman, with the added knowledge of a fine industrial mechanic and modelmaker. He must know how to handle materials on the lathe, soldering, welding and other industrial processes. (L. Moholy-Nagy, *Vision in Motion*, p. 235.)

The new technical means, while derived from industry, are not necessarily limited to the terms of industry. The distinction seems to be of purpose. Both the sculptor and the mechanic are involved with the manipulation of crude materials to make a desired object. Both must have considerable experience with

Jack Mays, sculptor. Photo by Natalie Townes.

material and technique; the nature and function of that experience, however, are what distinguish the two. The mechanic is concerned with the production of an object for use — its value and purpose is essentially instrumental. The purpose of the artist's production is the achievement of qualitative values in and for themselves, with no other purpose.

Involvement with Materials

In the Bauhaus in Germany and later at the School of Design in Chicago, teaching in the visual arts concentrated on the materials of art, their physical properties and potentialities for expression. Primary emphasis was placed upon the potential that each material, by its physical nature, had for plastic organization. The student was encouraged to take a material or group of materials and through experimentation discover the many possible ways in which they could be shaped. Involvement in depth with materials and technique in this manner not only provides opportunities to render expression but becomes a process of interaction where the student's base of intellectual and emotional concern is expanded. Moholy-Nagy set forth the following axiom:

The acquisition of technique and skills increases the expressive power of the individual; and with the accumulation of experiences his intellectual status is refined. This refinement in turn affects his emotional existence. (L. Moholy-Nagy, *Vision in Motion*, p. 35.)

By concentrating on materials themselves students develop a full, sensuous realization of their unique properties. In emphasizing the physical and sensory qualities of the various media, a point is established which can provide greater understanding of form, structure, and expression.

An inherent danger in this approach is that too great a concentration on tools, processes, and materials for their own sake will lead to an undesirable split between the technical aspects of a work of art and its expressive function. Mere technical achievement separated and studied for itself has no meaning or relevance to the personal vision and inner life of the student.

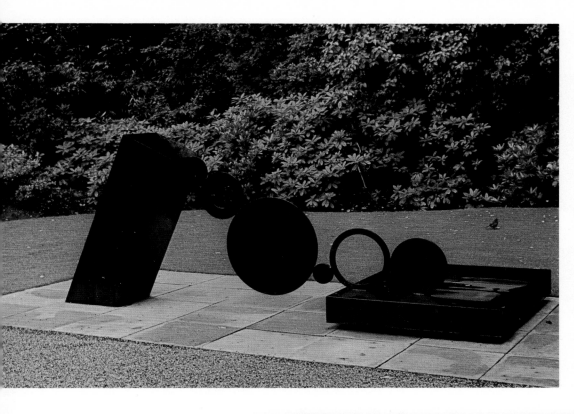

Brian Wall,
Six Circles, 1966.
Painted steel.

Phillip King,
Slant, 1965.
Arborite. 72″ high.

27

Acquiring Skills and Techniques

Experiences designed for the student of sculpture today cannot be bound at the outset by a formalized technique o series of procedures imposed by tradition and convention. He must be encouraged to explore his own unique idea, to play with a series of individually determined forms and solution which evolve primarily out of feeling. As his form begins to emerge he must learn to recognize its need for modification expansion, or redirection in terms of his materials and meth ods. Cumulative knowledge in this sense has an important place in the shaping of a sculptor. His capacity for expression is directly related to his understanding of and skill in manipu lating materials and tools. This does not, however, indicate the necessity for formal training in skills and techniques prio to or apart from the student's involvement with expression To practice formal technique without regard for expressive purposes runs counter to the natural order of the artistic process. The results of practice for skill development and ex perimentation by the sculptor are in many ways similar to the drawings and sketches by painters — often highly expressive in a limited context.

The contemporary sculptor is first concerned with the achievement of articulate expression; skills and techniques, o the "craft" of sculpture, make up his personal vocabulary. The traditions and limitations from sculpture of the past, its train ing procedures and disciplines cannot provide solutions o adequate expressive means for the sculptor today.

Structuring of experiences is dependent upon the individua and his unique expressive purposes and must originate from within the student himself. Essential to an understanding and appreciation of sculpture for the practitioner is mastery of it technical aspects. A knowledge of and skill with the tools o sculpture, its techniques and the way it is made is at the base of such understanding.

Considerations regarding the nature of the material, it processes and technical aspects are interwoven with aesthetic

Edward Higgins, *Untitled,* 1966. Welded steel and epoxy, 65" x 20" x 11". Courtesy of Leo Castelli Gallery, New York. Photo by Rudolph Burckhardt.

considerations. The directions the sculptor follows, or the sculptural problems he sets for himself, are to a large degree predetermined by his understanding of the relationship between these considerations. A path between two poles must be carefully navigated. On the one hand a sculptor must develop skills and abilities with which to work his material; he must overcome technical problems in order to avoid situations in which the medium controls the manipulator. Shoddy or inept craftsmanship seldom permits full realization of the sculptor's form concept. Sculpture demands structural adequacy, it must hold together and support itself. On the other hand, as previously stated, highly developed skills and complete mastery of material and technique may lead to mere exhibitionism. The sculptor, overly impressed with the technical, then becomes what Herbert Read calls a "virtuoso":

. . skill in Art is usually subordinate to the artist's intention. I say usually because there is an exceptional type of artist whose only purpose is to display his technical skill; with him the means becomes the end. We call him a virtuoso and he is apt to be a very inferior kind of artist. (Herbert Read, *The Art of Sculpture*, p. 33.)

A paradox confronts the neophyte sculptor seeking those experiences which will best prepare him in his craft. A rigorous technical training or an apprenticeship under a master sculptor would be an invaluable source of information; it might also restrict his own inventiveness. A tendency to follow pat solutions or tried and proven methods often results from such an emphasis. In acquiring a thorough familiarity with the way certain materials have been used, a concept of their "proper" and "improper" applications, and a knowledge of their history and successful uses, the student may be more impressed by such factors than inherent potential. The other side of the paradox is obvious — the sculptor's inventiveness and ingenuity with a material or process is contingent upon his backlog of knowledge and experiences.

Don Irving, *Growth Form*, 1961. Steel, 74" high. Collection of Mr. & Mrs. Peter Moore.

James Seawright, *Watcher*, 1966. Metal, plastic, electronic parts, 37" high x 30" diameter. Collection of Mr. & Mrs. Howard Lipman. Courtesy of Stable Gallery, New York. Photo by John D. Schiff.

A Personal Style

Individual interests and experiences of the student often lead to unique form problems and indicate approaches for their solution. Components of the student's lived world, natural or man-made, conceptual or physical, are the "stuff" from which his art is constructed. It is when images and media are united in ways significant to his individually determined direction that purely formal considerations have most meaning. Design factors, tensional forces, juxtapositions of light and weight, and a myriad of technical considerations contribute to the concreteness of the final object. In facing such problems the student is confronted with a situation each sculptural innovator of the past and present has faced. The manner in which they approached their problems and the form inventions which resulted can be both guide and inspiration. In this context the study of past and current works of sculpture has a direct and fruitful bearing on studio experiences.

An outstanding example of innovation, the electronic sculpture of James Seawright results from a range of unique concerns and experiences which led him to introduce radically new materials and concepts into sculpture. His background as an engineering officer in the U. S. Navy, a stage technician,

and an instructor-technician at the Columbia-Princeton Electronic Music Center all contributed to the formulation of unique (form) problems. He collaborated with his wife, a dancer, and the choreographer Alwin Nikolais to deal in imaginative ways with the fusion of movement, light, and electronic music.

The structures which resulted from the pursuit of his interests and concerns have changed the notion that sculpture is restricted to a time or place. These automated structures, made of metal, plastic, and electronic parts, buzz, light up, and travel paths that are determined in part by available light. When several of his pieces are placed together in a room the light-producing and light-sensing components of the structures are capable of modifying their own programs of movement and sound. They allow a continually varying pattern of activity within each work and among works. Such activity is not unrelated to dance movements.

It is clearly incumbent upon each artist that he draw from his own private world those impressions, skills, and concerns which move him and that he find resources essential to making valid art in the elements and materials which make up the external world. A personal idiom or style is very often determined by the qualities and potential of the industrial methods and materials discovered and applied by the sculptor in his experimentation. He has access to many and diverse approaches — and welding and the use of molten metals permit him to revise and supplement.

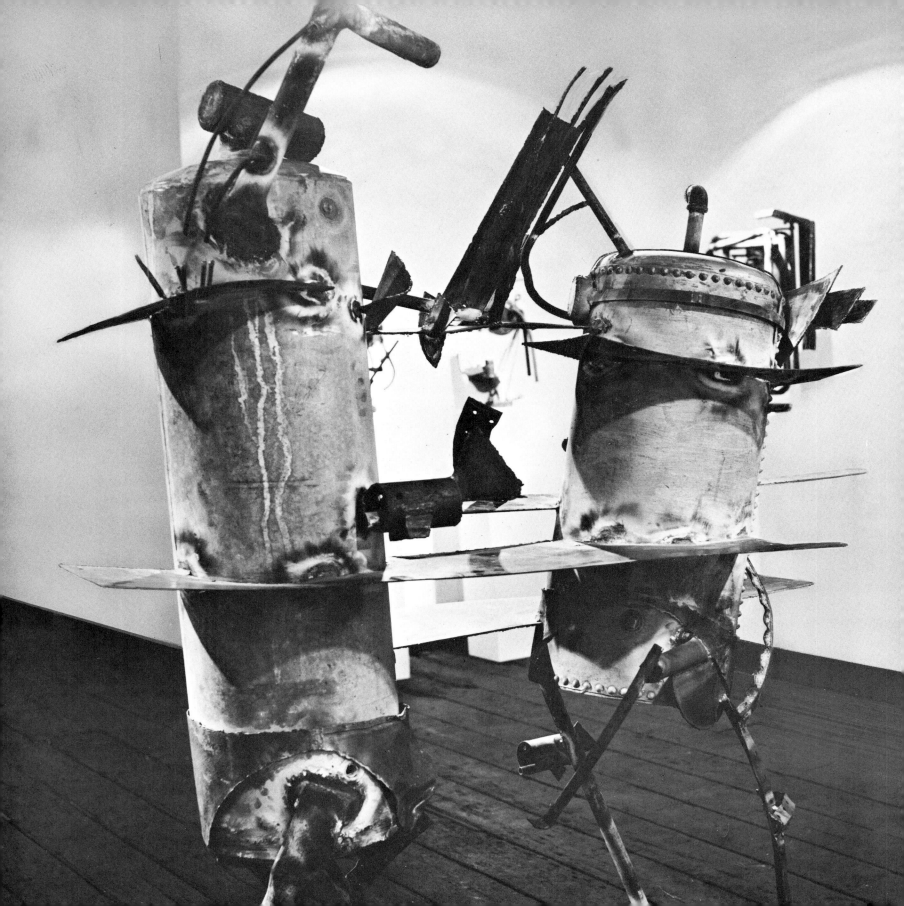

The ease with which metal parts may be joined permanently by welding is illustrated in the sculpture of Stankiewicz. *Playful Bathers* is an assemblage of found objects, or junk, joined permanently by welding. His selection of cast-off parts, still reminiscent of their former life, contributes to the lyrical, often humorous quality of Stankiewicz's sculpture. A distinct group of contemporary sculptors work in this manner, attempting to find a new life of form for one aspect of our visual environment, using the "stuff" of that environment.

Smith, who used a similar joining process, referred to his sculpture as "fabrications." His structures were most frequently built up from standard metal stock which had been cut, forged, or otherwise shaped to fit his personal image. Smith's *Lecturn Sentinel* is an example of such fabrication of stainless steel sheet in which the pieces were cut to measure, fitted, and joined by welding. While Smith pre-forms shapes and otherwise treats his material in developing his sculpture, the materials are allowed to assert themselves powerfully. He emphasizes the raw structural qualities and permanency of his media; mass and surface are diminished in favor of perforation and movement.

Opposite
Richard Stankiewicz, *Playful Bathers*, 1960. Iron and steel, 80" x 76" x 29". Courtesy of Stable Gallery, New York.

Right
David Smith, *Lecturn Sentinel*, 1961. Stainless steel, 101³/₄" x 33" x 20¹/₂". Collection of Whitney Museum of American Art, New York, Gift of the Friends of American Art. Photo by Geoffrey Clements.

Don Irving,
Female Form, 1962. Steel, 62".

him to work with authority, infusing an inorganic material with vitality and dynamic life. The sculpture exudes energy and force, unfolding and absorbing space. Some edges and surfaces were ground, filed, and polished, adding a reflective sparkle at carefully reasoned junctures.

Lassaw has conducted numerous experiments melting metal over an armature. He has used steel, nickel, silver, copper, brass, and phosphor bronze in this manner. *Enactment* was "built up by accretion, one drop of metal melted on another." As the form emerged, heavier sections were developed, adding

Opposite
Ibram Lassaw, *Enactment*, 1961. Bronze alloys, copper, and steel, 25" x 20" x 12". Collection, Mr. & Mrs. Howard Lipman.

Theodore J. Roszak, *Spectre of Kitty Hawk,* 1946-47. Welded and hammered steel brazed with bronze and brass, 40¼" high. Collection, The Museum of Modern Art, New York. Purchase.

Closely related to the joining process is the fabrication of the many-faceted surface, illustrated in *Female Form.* For this figure, thin sheet steel was cut with an automatic shear into predetermined shapes and joined by a welded bead, which provided the accent for change in direction of the surface planes. Masses and volumes of the sculpture were developed in this manner. Surfaces were engineered for structural strength, relying on the welded bead connections rather than an interior skeletal support.

Modeling directly in metals, treating them as plastic, malleable materials, is a truly contemporary approach to metalworking. The sculptor equipped with an oxy-acetylene welding torch has a degree of control over molten metal which combines great flexibility with ease of handling. Roszak used such a technique in his *Spectre of Kitty Hawk.* This sculpture was built up of steel rod, plate, wire, and other stock which was fused into a homogeneous mass. Roszak's absolute mastery of the technique of modeling steel in its molten plastic state freed

structural support to the work. His manner of working is much like building sand castles, where wet sand is dripped and built up in small gobs.

The wire sculptures of Lippold are intricately precise tension structures. *Bird of Paradise III* is an example of such structure. Constructed of nickel, chromium, and stainless steel wire and containing several hundred brazed or welded joints, it is a superb example of the refinement possible using the equipment and technique of industry.

A method of working sheet stock using an automatic shear

has been developed by Ferber. Shapes from sheet copper o brass, usually long, curved, or angular strips, are jointed by brazing to form the main elements of an open-space structure Ferber continues by cutting away some parts, adding others developing textures of melted alloys, and attaching small clus ters of rod. The sculpture *Homage to Piranesi I* was developed in this manner. The processes and techniques Ferber used are a result of many years of experimenting with soldering, braz ing, and welding. His forms are a direct result of such experi mentation with industrial materials and techniques.

Opposite
Richard Lippold, *Bird of Paradise III*, 1964.
Collection, Nelson A. Rockefeller. Courtesy of
Willard Gallery, New York. Photo by
Charles Uht.

Right
Herbert Ferber, *Homage to Piranesi I*, 1962–63.
Welded and brazed sheet copper and brass
tubing, 91¼" high x 48¾" width x 47⅞".
Collection, The Museum of Modern Art, New
York. Photo by Eric Pollitzer.

Robert Israel, *Suspended Floating Environment*, December 1967-January 1968. Plastic. Courtesy of Walker Art Center, Minneapolis, Minnesota.

THE ULTRA-CONCEPTUAL APPROACH — Among developments in the visual arts of the 1960s is the ultra-conceptual approach that emphasizes the designing process almost exclusively. The emotional-intuitive processes in which the sculptor responds directly to his materials and invents techniques responsive to his concept is rejected by some artists, who emphasize the thinking process almost exclusively. Their work, designed in the studio but executed elsewhere by professional craftsmen, removes them from contact with the physical evolution of a work of art. The art object is simply the end product of an idea or concept and it is the concept which is of greatest significance. The studio becomes a library of technical manuals and production reports where the artist acts as coordinator and organizer. Some observers of the contemporary scene see in these developments a profound de-materialization of art as object; others have even predicted a time when the art object as we have known it in museums and galleries will be obsolete, to be replaced by disposable objects or visual images which may be re-created when desired by electronic devices.

Robert Israel created an environment at The Walker Art

Center in Minneapolis where forty inflated tubes, each sixty feet long, were suspended on a series of slings. Each tube could be varied by adjusting ropes changing its shape. Color and size were also adjustable. When the exhibition was over the objects were deflated, stored, or discarded. The entire project could be re-created according to plan at a future date.

In the reductive sculpture of Donald Judd we can see a preoccupation with new materials, often synthetic, which possess none of the historical connotations of marble, wood, or bronze. Nor do they evoke the many often-romantic associations of carving techniques or casting processes so significant in traditional sculpture. Earlier twentieth-century styles which emphasized struggle and expressive involvement are eliminated. Processes and materials are adapted from their role in advanced technology and in the final work no trace of the creative process is discernible.

Such art must originate as a clear and unifying concept directly and at the beginning, not as the result of refining a technique through a number or works to arrive at the essence of an idea. The conception of a work is completely realized before it is made. Assistants or technicians in a factory execute construction or fabrication stages from drawings and their work is not allowed to affect the plan for the completed sculpture. The artistic achievement thus resides in the quality of the original conception. The idea must be motivated and guided by a distinct sensitivity which is often the primary attribute of much of the new sculpture. Realizing the idea involves the sculptor in many critical and essential choices at an early stage — scale, proportion, material and color, all essential to a

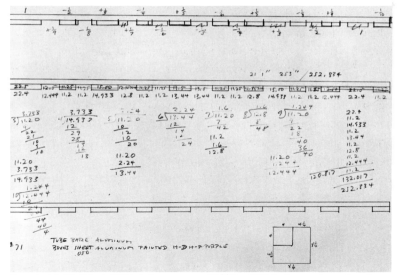

Don Judd, *Untitled*, 1965. Ink on paper, 16³/₄″ x 21³/₄″. Preparatory drawing for *Untitled*, 1966. Painted aluminum, 8¹/₄″ x 253″ x 8¹/₄″. Collection, Mr. & Mrs. Larry Zox. Photo by Geoffrey Clements.

realization of the intensity and purity of the original concept, must be all worked out before any physical work is done.

An approach to sculpture which separates the concept and production has obvious limitations. In some instances, technology suitable to the artist's conceptions is not available and must be invented. For a number of years sculptors had expressed an interest in developing non-material three-dimensional forms. They experimented with light-refracting techniques, controlled air-flow and smoke. When scientists used laser beams to produce three-dimensional images, called holograms, such immaterial sculpture became entirely possible.

Don Judd, *Untitled*, 1965. Aluminum and anodized aluminum, 8¹/₄″ x 253″ x 8¹/₄″. Collection of Whitney Museum of American Art, New York, Gift of Howard and Jean Lipman Foundation, Inc. Photo by Geoffrey Clements.

The sculptor who does not have access to the experimental laboratory or an opportunity to share his ideas with an engineer, who tries to generate ideas significant to contemporary life from a position of isolation, has great difficulty avoiding tendencies to gimmickry in adapting the products of technology to his work. Collaborations between artists and engineers have produced happenings, environments, and objects which are precursors of significant developments in the visual arts.

An organization called Experiments in Art and Technology, Incorporated, was formed with the express purpose of bringing together artists and engineers to contribute to the evolution of a work of art.

The decision to form Experiments in Art and Technology, Incorporated, developed from the experience of producing the performance series, "9 Evenings: Theatre and Engineering," which was held at the 69th Regiment Armory in New York in October 1966. Forty engineers and ten well-known, avant-garde artists worked together to develop technical equipment which was used as an integral part of the theater, dance and music works. During the preparations for "9 Evenings" it became clear that if a continuing and organic artist-engineer relationship was to be achieved, a major organized effort had to be made to set up the necessary physical and social conditions.

In November, 1966, a meeting was held for artists in New York City to find out if E.A.T. as an organization could work to provide the artists with access to the technical world. Over 300 artists, engineers, and other interested people attended and the reaction was positive. Billy Kluver, a physicist in laser research at Bell Labs, became President, and Robert Rauschenberg, artist, Vice-President. Membership was opened to all artists and engineers.

To involve the artist with the relevant forces shaping the technological world, the artist must have access to the people who are creating technology. Thus it was decided that E.A.T. act as a matching agency, through which an artist with a technical problem or a technologically complicated and advanced project be put in touch with an engineer or scientist who could collaborate with him. E.A.T. not only matches artists and engineers to work on collaborative projects but also works to secure industrial sponsorship for the projects that result from the collaboration.

E.A.T. aims to involve industry and also to gain the interest and support of other institutions in society: universities, foundations, labor, even politics. These broad contacts will cut across traditional boundaries and facilitate the completion of projects initiated by the artist-engineer collaboration. E.A.T. is founded on the strong belief that an industrially sponsored, effective working relationship between artists and engineers will lead to new possibilities which will benefit society as a whole.   *E.A.T. News*, Vol. 2, No. 1 (March 18, 1968), p. 2.

The Studio

A sculptor's studio is a very personal place reflective of his manner of working and his concerns. It is often filled with inspirational material collected from a variety of sources. Lee Bontecou, an amateur biologist, has surrounded herself with a large collection of organic forms and specimens, shells of crustaceans, sun bleached skulls, butterflies — an interest which has begun to be reflected in her recent work. David Smith's studio was located on a farm at Bolton Landing, New York, and he called it "the Terminal Iron Works," after a former studio location in New York City. Indeed it resembled an iron works with its heavy industrial equipment for moving his large steel structures. Smith subscribed to a number of technical journals and the resource library in his studio contained many up-to-date reports of developments in the steel industry.

Fountain detail.

Bertoia fountain commissioned for city of Philadelphia (in progress).

41

Patina and washing area.

Studio of Harry Bertoia with raised asbestos-covered platform for welding.

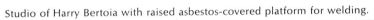

Many studios are large open spaces, warehouse lofts or industrial buildings and kept flexible enough in arrangement to prepare a special set of circumstances conducive to the development of an idea or project. The prime requirement of a studio is that it be a functional place suited to the way an artist works. Some studios are cluttered, with materials and tools scattered about. Others, like that of Harry Bertoia, are well ordered and carefully arranged. Bertoia's studio has been set up in a converted automobile repair garage, well suited to the needs of a sculptor-welder. His aim in organizing the studio is to keep it as flexible as possible — spaces are divided by movable partitions within which he can create an environment for a piece as it develops. When he is working on a sculpture, the visual field must be free and uncluttered by objects and projects not related to it. Separate areas are established for certain operations and only the tools and equipment needed for the work in progress are allowed to intrude. An acid bath and washing area equipped with floor drain and rubber mats occupy one corner of the large building. Storage bins and racks line one wall and contain a wide variety of wire, bar and sheet stock of steel, brass, bronze, and aluminum, all carefully labeled. A raised platform in the center of the studio covered with asbestos sheet acts as a working stage where the sculptor can isolate a work or series of works in progress. A bench at the back of the studio is used for most brazing operations. It is equipped with a large hood and exhaust system to carry off the noxious fumes of molten brass or bronze.

Harry Bertoia started in the visual arts as a jeweler. He indicated that his jewelry "kept getting larger and larger." This early training as a craftsman and his commitment to a personally evolved craft of sculpture is reflected in the order of his working surroundings.

At the time of a recent visit to his studio he was nearing completion of a major work, a fountain for the city of Philadelphia. His discussion of that work provides many insights to his approach.

In his early considerations of the problem of a fountain sculpture he rejected casting as a process in favor of the direct approach of welding, which "hides nothing," where "growth is in the spirit of the thing." He wanted to control the sculpture from start to finish, and as he worked the configuration of the masses and shapes kept changing daily. "The heat of the day

Brazing area with large exhaust system and hood overhead.

Studio of sculptor Kahil Gibran.

Collection of found objects and scrap metal in studio storage area.

or a cool breeze affected its development; if I were not in complete control, these factors would not contribute." The fountain is constructed of 1-inch-diameter heavy wall copper tubing, heated, shaped, and welded. He has assistants to help him with some operations, but if he is not present, "not a single tube would be added." The fountain was outside at the back to the studio for it was too large and heavy to be constructed inside. However an earlier commission of large proportions was constructed in the building and portions of the roof had to be removed to make room for it.

Cost was also a factor in this project. Bertoia compared his fountain with the Henry Moore *Figure* which had just been installed at the Lincoln Center for the Performing Arts in New York City. The *Figure* cost more than $80,000 to cast, while the cost of fabrication of Bertoia's fountain was less than $20,000. Although comparable in size, it has a larger overall surface area.

Kahil Gibran's studio is on the street floor of his remodeled town house in Boston's South End. The main studio room is large and well organized, containing a carefully identified collection of rusted and twisted metal pieces collected over the years from junk yards, secondhand stores, and the streets of Boston. The character of the metal, its texture and patina often suggests an application, as the curls of rusted metal for hair or deteriorated length of structural steel as arrow shaft. He makes a majority of his tools and equipment himself to solve

Metal-working tools reminiscent of blacksmith shop.

Figure in process, welded steel.

specific construction or forging problems. Tongs, pincers, forging stakes, and hammers fashioned out of steel have much of the quality of a blacksmith's equipment, but the clean, precise and orderly studio reflects the careful control this sculptor exerts over his material and processes.

Gibran, a master craftsman in complete control of a contemporary medium, has applied oxy-acetylene welding techniques to increase his facility for dealing with established concepts in sculpture. In 1954 he developed a technique of welding wire to describe, with anatomical precision, the straining figure of John the Baptist. In a later development, wire was combined with forged steel for *Figure*, in which the hard recalcitrant qualities of sheet steel are transformed with incredible facility to the folds and flow of leather or fabric.

BASIC CONSIDERATIONS — A fluid work space often revolves around a project, the work in progress changing the character of the environment as it develops. With the expanding dimensions of much contemporary work, size of the work space is a significant factor. Small spaces can be restrictive and limiting while overly large spaces can be overpowering and wasted. Ample space for storing material, tools, and completed work should be considered, even a display area for finished sculpture may be possible. Physical or mechanical factors often need to be adjusted. It is frustrating, for example, to blow fuses continually because of inadequate wiring or to have to use a sink in another room because of limited plumbing. Often additions can be made at relatively little expense which greatly increase the utility of a work space. Large doors with access for loading will facilitate shipping and receiving materials and sculpture. Floors must be capable of supporting the weight of the largest piece anticipated, overhead beams or tracks for chain hoists are a distinct advantage in handling large or heavy pieces. Hygroscopic materials, plaster, or cement require a storage place that is dry, while clay or plaster works in progress must be kept damp for long periods of time.

Light is a matter of personal preference, but in addition to whatever natural or artificial lighting is available, movable floods and spot lights can be installed to light a piece in the same way it will be exhibited in a gallery or museum. Most galleries now use recessed spots in the ceiling and light sculpture from directly overhead.

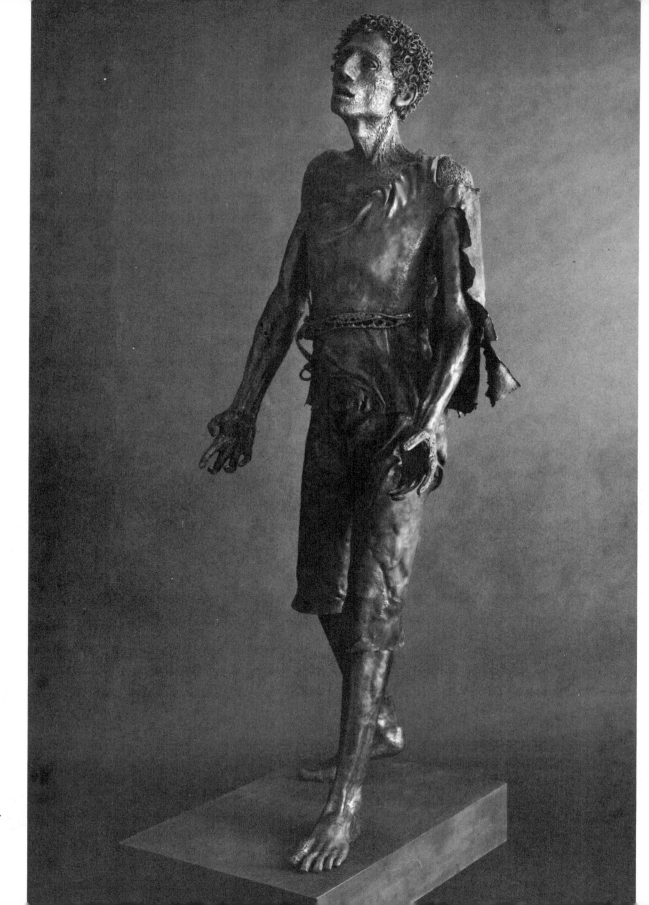

Kahil Gibran, *Figure*. Welded steel.
Photo by Stephen F. Grone.

Robert Murray, *Duet*, 1965. Steel, 18' x 4' x 10'. Courtesy of Bethlehem Steel Corporation. Sculpture on site at Long Beach State College, California.
Photo by Harry Merrick.

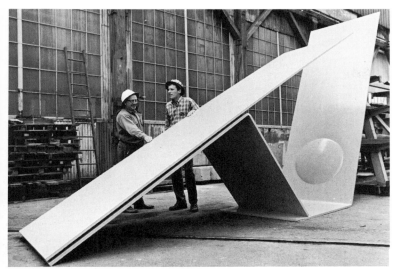

Robert Murray with Fergus McKay, foreman of the structural fabricating department at Bethlehem Steel Corporation's San Pedro Yard, where the sculpture *Duet* was fabricated from steel plate. Photo by Bethlehem Steel.

posium in which eight sculptors participated. They were given the opportunity to work in factories with materials and technical assistance provided. Robert Murry worked at Bethlehem Steel to produce *Duet* with the cooperation of workmen. He was able to oversee the execution of his work and apply mass production techniques in making a unique object.

Robert Murray, *Dyad*, 1966. Aluminum painted with dark blue epoxy, 16½' high. Constructed by the Aluminum Welding Co. of Montreal. Located at the Arrival Plaza Ile Notre Dame (Expo '67). Courtesy of Betty Parsons Gallery, New York.

Working in the Factory

Many contemporary sculptors who use the materials and techniques of industry have moved outside their own studios into shops and factories for the construction or fabrication of sculpture. Industry has the necessary facilities, machinery, technicians, and know-how to deal with mass production techniques. A nearly limitless selection of structural shapes and stock parts are readily available in the warehouses of an industrial complex. A well-equipped metal working shop or factory can perform highly sophisticated operations with power shears, bending brake, stamp, and power forge. Therefore, many sculptors have found that a practical solution to technical problems is to work in direct collaboration with shops and factories.

In 1965 Long Beach State College, with the cooperation of a number of California industries, sponsored a sculpture sym-

Kowalski with *Dynamite* on site at
Long Beach State College, California.

Above and right
Explosive forming procedure at El Toro High Energy Forming Facility,
North American Rockwell Corporation.

   Piotr Kowalski in collaboration with North American Avia-
tion, Inc. employed advanced "explosive forming" techniques
to produce *Dynamite*. In this process explosive charges were
attached to a stainless steel sheet immersed in water and the
charges detonated to establish the shape.

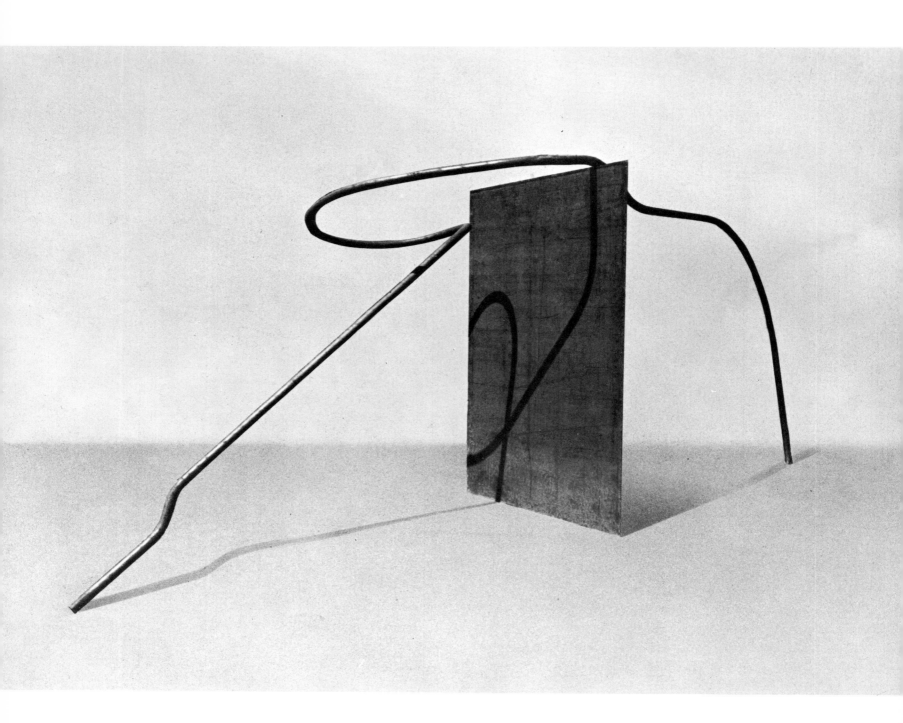

The sculptor of today has fallen heir to the new materials, techniques, and influences of industry. From the enormous resources of the technical world he has made selections, devised new combinations, adopted unorthodox methods and developed remarkable innovations to achieve his unique purposes. In each case, however, the sculptor has had to explore for himself the relationship between his concept and the means by which his ideas are expressed. The student of sculpture has no less a problem.

Opposite
Alexander Liberman, *Trace*, 1967. Steel, 8'2" x 22'7" x 6'. Courtesy of Andre Emmerich Gallery.

Right
John Chamberlain, *Velvet White*, 1962. Welded steel, 83" x 57" x 48". Collection, Mr. & Mrs. Albert A. List. Photo, Rudolph Burkhardt.

John Chamberlain, *Madam Moon*, 1964. Polychrome welded steel, 19" x 29" x 21". Courtesy of Mr. & Mrs. Robert Rowan, Pasadena, California.

54

Welding and Brazing

4

The direct metal techniques of welding and related techniques of soldering and brazing are processes used extensively in industrial production and repair. Applications range from underwater welding for repair and salvage operations to computerized arc welding machines in use on modern assembly lines. Many types of welding and brazing rod alloys have been developed to meet exacting requirements and specific industrial applications. Precise technical information is available from most manufacturers and suppliers of welding equipment. However, the sculptor is not concerned with such technical specifications, except in rare instances. His concern is the proficient use of his equipment and materials to achieve a wide variety of visual and tactile effects. Where the technician would seek to eliminate the jagged edge left by the cutting torch, the sculptor might find intriguing sculptural possibilities in this characteristic. The mechanic often attempts to remove all traces of the process by grinding off the typical bead; the sculptor on the other hand frequently exploits such qualities and incorporates them as an integral part of his finished product.

Automated welder. Courtesy of General Motors Corporation.

Oxy-Acetylene Welding

The incredible versatility of oxy-acetylene welding coupled with the efficiency, simplicity, and direct nature of the process make it one of the most widely used sculptural techniques today. It is essentially a method of joining metal by melting and fusing into a homogeneous mass both parent metals and filler. A limited section of the metals to be joined is heated to the melting point by a concentrated flame of oxygen and acetylene properly mixed in a welding torch. A puddle of molten metal is thus developed and fed by a rod of filler metal. As the work proceeds, the puddle cools and solidifies into the characteristic bead.

EQUIPMENT — Basic welding and cutting apparatus satisfactory for performing most of the operations of the welder-sculptor consists of the following:

Tanks — Two steel-cylinder, high-pressure tanks, one oxygen and one acetylene, which may be leased or rented from a welding supply house.

Regulators — two pressure regulators or reducing valves, one oxygen and one acetylene gas. For most studio requirements the two-stage type regulator is preferred because it provides a more uniform gas flow. In the two-stage regulator the reduction of cylinder pressure to that required at the torch is accomplished through two pressure chambers inside the unit. The gas passes into the high pressure chamber where a predetermined pressure is maintained (normally 200 pounds per square inch for oxygen and 50 pounds per square inch for acetylene). From the high-pressure chamber the gas passes into a second chamber where it is released into the hose line by means of an adjusting screw. Both regulators have two pressure gauges; one indicates pressure in the cylinder and the other shows the working pressure delivered at the blowpipe.

Hoses — A specially designed non-porous hose should be used with welding equipment. A double hose joined by a web is preferred. Green is the standard color for oxygen and red for acetylene. This color code, while not uniform, normally applies to regulators and tanks as well. Connections on the oxygen hose regulator and valves utilize a normal or right-hand thread while the acetylene connections may be identified by a

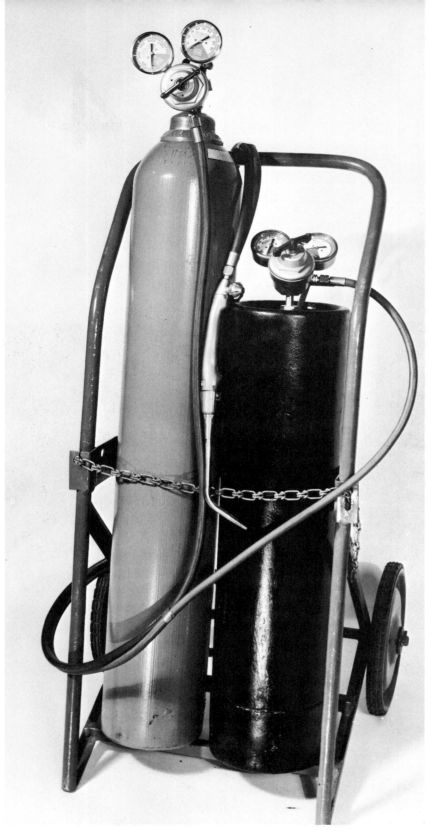

Oxy-acetylene welding and cutting outfit on truck.
Courtesy of Union Carbide Corporation.

56

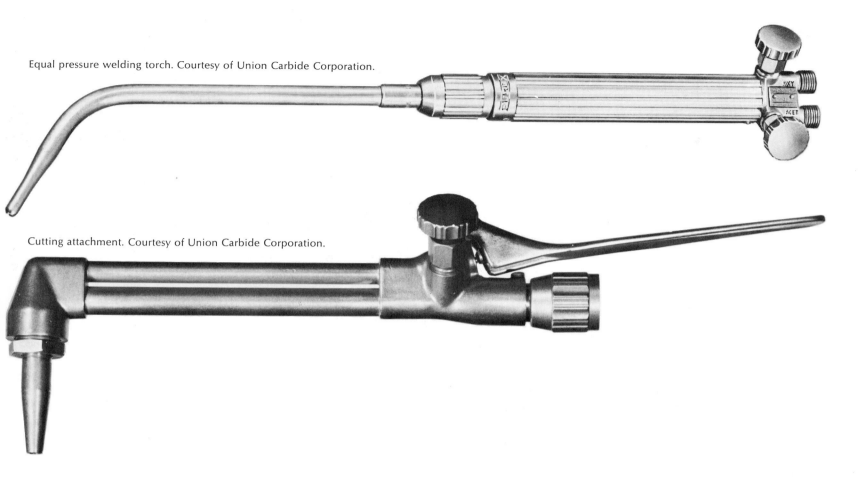

Equal pressure welding torch. Courtesy of Union Carbide Corporation.

Cutting attachment. Courtesy of Union Carbide Corporation.

groove in the connector nut indicating a left-hand thread.

Blowpipe or torch and cutting attachment — The blowpipe should be carefully selected. It is the instrument in the hands of the sculptor as he works, therefore weight, balance, and performance are prime considerations. The blowpipe receives gasses through needle valves from the two regulators, mixes them and delivers a uniform mixture at even pressure to produce a proper welding flame. There are many types of blow-pipes available. Generally, they are classified according to the relative pressure of oxygen and acetylene. The "low pressure" or "injector" types are designed to use acetylene at very low pressure (1 pound per square inch or less); "balanced pressure" or "equal pressure" types are most often used in the production of sculpture and have the greatest versatility (acety-lene pressures from 1 pound per square inch to 15 pounds per square inch). Practically all welding blowpipes are provided

with a series of interchangeable tips of varying sizes to extend the range and variety of operations using the same handle. Manufacturers specifications packed with the blowpipe indi-cate the correct size tip to select for welding metal of a given thickness. Size of the tip, thickness of the metal to be welded, and pressure of the welding gasses must be coordinated in the welding operation. The most flexible arrangement for oxy-acetylene cutting is the attachment which can be fitted directly to the blowpipe handle by a hand-tight connector nut. Such arrangements allow the sculptor to change from a welding to cutting operation with relative ease. In the cutting blowpipe the oxy-acetylene flame is produced through a series of small holes surrounding a larger central opening. The flame pro-duced preheats the metal to bright red, at which point the cutting jet of oxygen is delivered through the central opening in the cutting tip.

Points to test for leakage.
Courtesy of Union Carbide Corporation.

Goggles — Eyes must be protected from the intensive light rays, heat, and sparks produced by the welding process. Special lenses are made for this purpose from colored optical glass that reduces the effect of glare and at the same time permits the sculptor to see his work clearly.

Friction spark lighter — The spark lighter is preferable for lighting the blowpipe. Hand-held matches are dangerous when used to light the oxy-acetylene flame.

Gloves — Gauntlet-type leather or asbestos gloves are recommended. They should be kept free of oil or grease when used with oxy-acetylene equipment.

Protective clothing — As the metal is heated to its molten state sparks are invariably given off, so suitable protection for clothing is required. Sweaters and other loosely woven woolen or synthetic garments should never be worn while welding. Hard surface denim or cotton twill shop coats or coveralls are satisfactory; a skull cap or hair covering is also recommended.

Wrenches — Multi-purpose open-ended wrenches of correct size are usually supplied with the equipment. Most fittings on regulators and blowpipes are of brass and are easily damaged if a pliers or oversized wrench is used.

Related equipment — The studio of the welder-sculptor will contain many additional pieces of equipment and hand tools selected as a result of a personal way of working. A well-equipped studio would probably include a brick or asbestos working surface, a variety of metal clamps, forging hammers and anvil, metal cutting devices, electric shear, bolt cutter, wire brushes, pliers, and water container.

ASSEMBLING THE APPARATUS — It is wise to establish a standard procedure in setting up the equipment for gas welding to insure its proper functioning and safe operation. The oxygen and acetylene cylinders should be securely fastened to a wall or column in the studio so that they will not tip or fall. Protective caps are then removed and the valves "cracked" to blow out and clean the valve outlets. Regulators, hose, and blowpipe handle may now be attached. You will recall that the acetylene fittings have a left-hand thread to prevent mixing the hoses and creating an explosive condition. (Note: Before attaching the blowpipe handle on new equipment, blow out the hoses to clear them of dust and other particles by releasing oxygen and acetylene under proper pressure.) All fittings should be firmly seated by using a snug wrench. With the regulator open, all connections under normal working pressure, and needle valves at the handle closed, run a test for leaks. Apply soapy water to all fittings. If bubbles form indicating a leak, tighten the connection. The following procedure for opening and closing down oxy-acetylene apparatus is recommended.

Opening: With the blowpipe needle valves open and the regulator diaphragm relaxed, slowly open the oxygen cylinder valve one full turn, and read the contents of the tank on the tank gauge. Using the same regulator and blowpipe settings, open the acetylene cylinder valve one-half turn; a reading will appear on that tank gauge also. Set both working pressures by adjusting the diaphragm screws until the correct readings appear on the pressure gauges. Immediately close the needle valves on the blowpipe. Normal welding pressures for acetylene range from 3 to 7 pounds per square inch — acetylene pressure should never exceed 15 pounds per square inch, welding pressures for oxygen normally range from 4 to 10 pounds per square inch. In the cutting operation, oxygen pressures range from 30 to 60 pounds while acetylene pressures generally remain below 8 pounds.

Closing: In shutting down the equipment for the day close the valves at both tanks first, then open the needle valves at the blowpipe handle to bleed the lines and relax pressure on the regulator diaphragms. When the two gauges on each regulater read "0" release the adjusting screw on the regulator and close the needle valves at the welding blowpipe.

The flame: To light the torch turn the acetylene on at the needle valve approximately three-quarters of a turn, and ignite it with a spark lighter. An orange flame will result, often producing quantities of black soot. With the acetylene burning, gradually open the oxygen needle valve until a clearly defined central cone surrounded by a second somewhat luminous blue cone is visible. This is the normal welding flame, called a neutral flame and composed of a one-to-one mixture of oxygen and acetylene. An excess of acetylene in the mixture will produce a reducing flame (also called a carbonizing flame); it is characterized by an intermediate flame area between the inner white cone and the blue outer envelope. A third kind of flame, called an oxidizing flame, is produced by forcing an excess of oxygen into the mixture. The white inner cone of flame reduces in size while the blue outer envelope deepens in hue and the burning is accompanied by a hiss or roar.

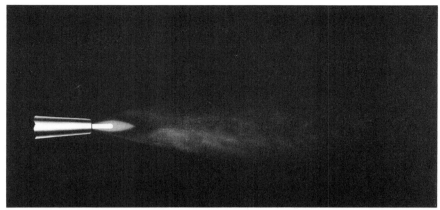

Excess acetylene flame. Courtesy of Union Carbide Corporation.

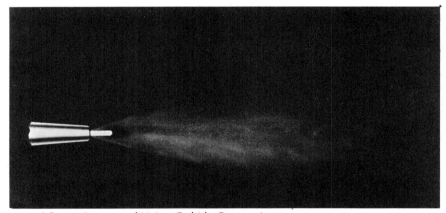

Neutral flame. Courtesy of Union Carbide Corporation.

Excess oxygen flame. Courtesy of Union Carbide Corporation.

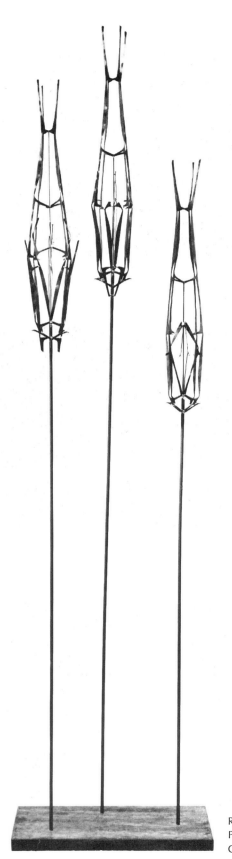

James Wines, *Suspended Disc #5*, 1966. Painted cement and steel, 88" x 60" x 18". Courtesy of Marlborough-Gerson Gallery, New York.

Rudy Wedow, *Seed Pods*, 1965.
Polished steel, 92¹/₂" x 20".
Courtesy of Mrs. Rudy Wedow.

BASIC TECHNIQUE — The technique for welding mild steel consists of melting both edges of the two parent metals simultaneously, causing them to flow together and solidify into a homogeneous mass. The torch should be lightly held and balanced in the hand, both to prevent fatigue and to allow for even movement. The hottest part of the flame is just ahead of the white cone. It should be held just off the steel at an approximate 30-degree angle pointing forward in the direction of the weld. In this manner excess flame will preheat the metal to be welded. The metal immediately under the flame will melt and form a puddle. By moving the torch slowly in a "U" or "O" rotation the puddle is continued for the length of the weld. The most common difficulty beginners have with the welding process is getting the metal hot enough and controlling the molten puddle. This is a relatively simple procedure requiring little practice to master but is an essential skill in producing a sound weld.

Steven Porter, *Flying High*, 1965. Painted steel, 39" x 70". Courtesy of Betty Parsons Gallery, New York.

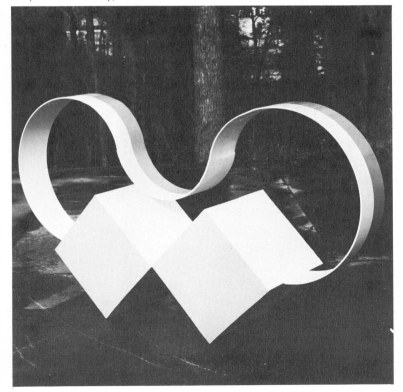

John Chamberlain, *Essex*, 1960. Welded metal, 108" x 90". Collection of the Museum of Modern Art, New York. Gift of Mr. & Mrs. Robert C. Scull. Courtesy of Leo Castelli Gallery, New York. Photo by Rudolph Burckhardt.

In most sculptural applications a filler rod will be required both to build up a joint and to fill gaps between two pieces of metal. The filler rod is normally of a diameter equal to the thickness of the parent metals; it is held at approximately the same angle as the torch but is slanted away from the torch. The tip of the filler rod should be kept in the center of the puddle and the flame directed at the base metal so that in effect the parent metal is being melted around the filler rod. If the rod slips out of the molten puddle, it will stick to the side, where the temperature is insufficient to melt it. To free the rod, play the flame directly on it; once it is free, re-form the puddle and move on. Practice will be required to move the puddle forward at the correct speed. If the movement is too slow, the puddle size increases and burn-through may result; if it is too fast the rod will not fuse with the parent metal but merely stick to the surface.

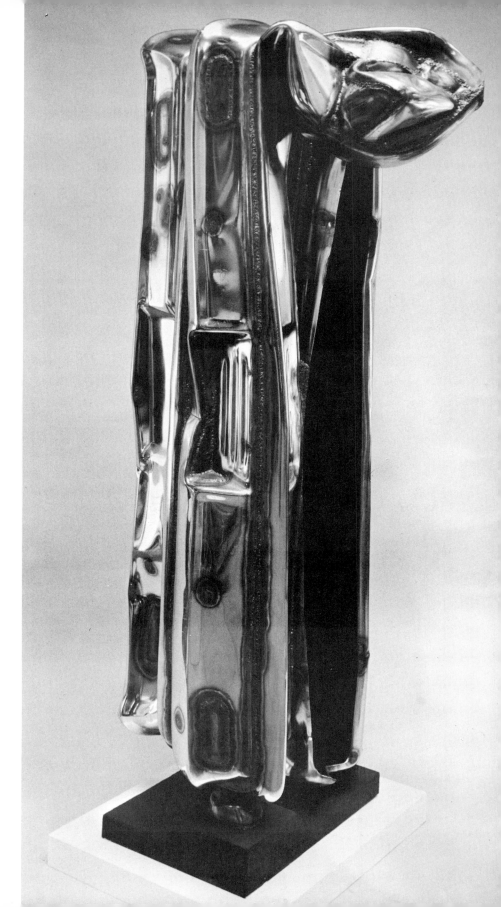

Right
Jason Seley, *Black on Chrome*, 1966. Chromium plated steel, 81" high. Courtesy of Kornblee Gallery, New York. Photo by Charles Uht.

Opposite
Lee Bontecou, *Untitled*, 1964. Welded steel with canvas, 21" x 17" x 6". Courtesy of Leo Castelli Gallery, New York.

Some faults: The following problems are common to beginning welder-sculptors: *Slag or brittle weld* results from improper flame adjustment. An excess oxygen or an oxidizing flame will burn steel, causing it to bubble and become brittle. *Burn-through* is caused by using too large a tip or holding the torch too long in one spot. *Flashback* results when the flame burns back into the torch with a hissing and squealing noise. A flashback may be caused by a clogged tip, damaged needle valves or improper pressure or backfire; the blowout of the flame is often followed by re-ignition. *Popping* occurs when the torch is operated at lower pressures than required by the size of the tip, when the tip is overheated, when it is touched to the work, or when an obstruction blocks the opening of the tip.

Mark Di Suvero, *Sliced Boilermaker*, 1966–67. Steel, 79" x 83" x 54". Courtesy of Paula J. Cooper. Photo by John D. Schiff.

Jack Rivers, *Welded Pipe Sections*, 1966. Steel, 36" high. Courtesy of the artist.

OXY-ACETYLENE PRESSURE FOR WELDING FERROUS METALS

TIP NO.	METAL THICKNESS (in.)	OXYGEN* PRESSURE (p.s.i.) APPROX.	ACETYLENE* PRESSURE (p.s.i.) APPROX.	ACETYLENE† CONSUMPTION (c.f.h.) APPROX.
00	1/64	1	1	0.5
0	1/32	1	1	1
1	1/16	1	1	2
2	3/32	2	2	5
3	1/8	3	3	9
4	3/16	4	4	16
5	1/4	5	5	25
6	5/16	6	6	30
7	3/8	7	7	40
8	1/2	7	7	60
9	5/8	7-1/2	7-1/2	70
10	3/4 up	9	9	90

* Pressures and consumptions shown are for separable tips with appropriate mixers. Operating pressures for tip-mixer assemblies to secure normal flow will be somewhat higher for the smaller sizes. Gas pressures are for hose lengths up to 25 feet. Increase pressure for longer length of hose.

† Oxygen consumption calculated at 1.1 times acetylene consumption.

NOTE: Never use grease or oil on any part of torch, cylinder valves or regulator. Tips must be used with proper size of mixer. Always blow out hoses after changing cylinders or equipment. Make up all connections with proper size wrenches, not gas pliers or Stillson wrenches.

WELDING ALUMINUM — Oxy-acetylene welding equipment may be used quite satisfactorily by the sculptor who finds aluminum most suited to a particular form or installation. Exterior applications, where weight and permanence in weather are important considerations, make aluminum a highly desirable material in the sculptor's inventory.

Techniques for welding aluminum combine elements of brazing, soldering, and steel welding processes. The oxy-acetylene flame produces sufficient heat to offset the high thermal conductivity of this material; however, preheating of the metal is often desirable, especially when joining thick sections. There are several excellent types of filler rod and wire available commercially, both bare and flux-coated. Pieces of the parent metal may also be used as filler. Aluminum should be backed or supported during the welding operation. There is no color change as the aluminum heats, and the high thermal conductivity of this materal may cause a sagging or burn-through if it is unsupported. The process for welding with gas flame requires that a flux be applied to the material used as filler and to the edges to be joined; flux protection is essential to prevent the development of scale or skin. When scale does develop, it acts as a container within which the aluminum melts, often resulting in burn-through. The size of the filler rod and its relationship to the thickness of the material being welded is more critical here than in other welding techniques. A rod that is too large will chill the puddle and build up in gobs. A reducing flame, one with a slight excess of acetylene, is recommended for most aluminum welding operations.

Cleaning of the material both before and after welding is important. Grease or oil may cause contamination of the weld and should be removed with commercial degreasing agents or acid. Thorough cleaning is also important *after* welding. Flux residues in combination with moisture are corrosive to aluminum and for this reason consideration should be given to a configuration which may be cleaned by immersion in a sulfuric acid bath (10 percent cold solution) and wire brushing with hot water.

When the joint to be welded has been properly prepared and fluxed, the slightly reducing flame of the torch is directed to the edge at the beginning of the weld to melt the flux. Scratch the melted flux with the filler rod while the flame is directed at the parent metal; continue this scratching until the

Robert Murray, *Track*, 1966. Steel and aluminum painted red, epoxy, 14½' long. Courtesy of Betty Parsons Gallery, New York.

Alexander Liberman, *Maquette for "Prometheus"*, 1963. Anodized aluminum, 60" high. Courtesy of Betty Parsons Gallery, New York. Photo by Hans Namuth.

filler metal melts and fuses with the base metal. The molten puddle of both base metal and filler is maintained as the weld advances. Forehand welding is generally best for welding aluminum since the flame preheats the area to be welded. The torch should be held at a slightly leading angle for thin material. For thicknesses above 3/16 inch, the torch may be held nearer the vertical to minimize the possibility of burning through.

OXY-ACETYLENE PRESSURES FOR WELDING ALUMINUM

TIP ORIFICE	METAL THICKNESS (in.)	OXYGEN PRESSURE (p.s.i.) APPROX.	ACETYLENE PRESSURE (p.s.i.) APPROX.
.031	1/16	2	2
.038	1/8	2	2
.046	3/16	3	3
.055	1/4	4	4
0.86	3/8	6	6
0.98	1/2	8	8

There is much confusion regarding the weldability of aluminum, due partially to the numerous alloys and surface treatments available. For most sculptural applications metals of high purity are best. Many sculptors who use aluminum will select one alloy and its appropriate filler rod and use that exclusively to avoid the frustrating experience of trying to weld incompatible alloys. Alloys which lend themselves particularly well to gas welding are: 1100 or 3003, used with 1100 filler rod; 5050, 5052, and 6061, used with 4043 filler rod (Aluminum Association designations).

WELDING STAINLESS STEEL — Numerous stainless steel alloys have been developed to meet a wide range of industrial and home applications. Their ability to resist corrosion even under the most severe conditions make them a desirable material for sculpture. The main constituents of stainless steel are iron, chromium, and nickel; the most common combination is referred to as 18-8 (approximately 18 percent chromium and 8 percent nickel). The American Iron and Steel Institute classi-

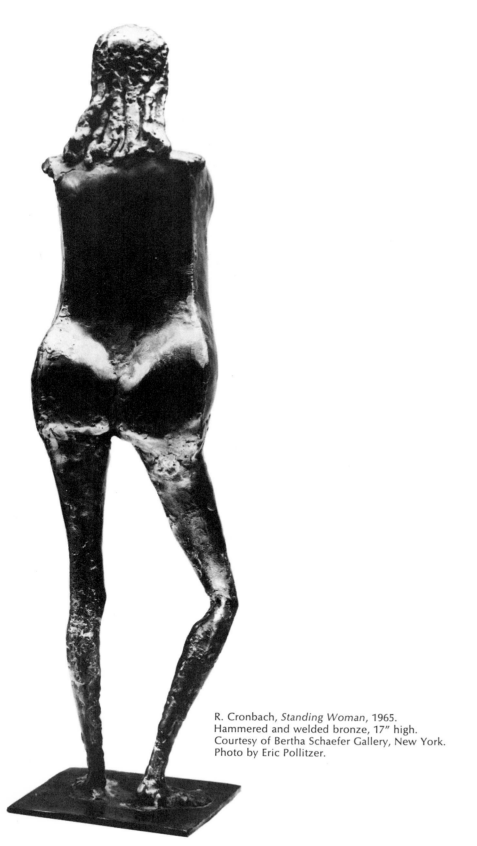

R. Cronbach, *Standing Woman*, 1965.
Hammered and welded bronze, 17" high.
Courtesy of Bertha Schaefer Gallery, New York.
Photo by Eric Pollitzer.

fies them into two general series — 300 and 400, each with appropriate sub-classifications. For the purposes of the sculptor the 300 series is generally preferable in that these steels have better welding qualities and require no annealing after welding. Oxy-acetylene welding is most effective on thickness less than 18 gauge; on heavier stock, inert-gas shielded-arc welding is recommended.

Stainless steel welding requires a technique similar to the standard welding process for mild steel. Select a tip that is two sizes smaller than the one used for mild steel of the same thickness. Since heat does not disperse as quickly from the weld zone of stainless steel, a smaller flame will insure against destroying the properties of the metal. A neutral flame is essential in welding stainless. Even a slight excess of oxygen may oxidize the chromium in the steel and reduce its corrosion-resistant qualities. Filler rods of specially treated columbium 18-8 are available and recommended for most applications. A rod of even higher chromium content is sometimes desirable since it will allow for the slight oxidation losses that occur. Chromium in stainless steel oxidizes quite easily and the oxide formed may act as a heat barrier. A flux is required to protect all heated surfaces from oxidation and to assist the flow characteristics of the metal.

WELDING BRONZE — Bronze is the metal most often used to cast sculpture. In recent years sculptors have rediscovered bronze as a sculptural medium and, perhaps because of technological advances and experiences with direct metal processes, they now work directly with the casting process in studio foundries. In most instances, sculptors will employ welding as a means of joining cast bronze elements, filling core pins, or rebuilding surfaces.

Bronze is essentially an alloy of copper, tin, lead, and zinc in various proportions — the traditional alloy is 85 and it is still used extensively. It consists of 85 percent copper, and 5 percent each of tin, lead, and zinc. The character of this metal which makes it a popular casting material also makes it comparatively easy to weld. A slightly oxidizing flame is used to reduce fumes and prevent boiling of the weld puddle. The flow characteristics of bronze may lead the sculptor to believe a flux is not necessary. However, oxides do form in the weld area and it is advisable to use a brazing flux, fused borax, or

Harris Barron, *Memphis*, 1962. Forged and welded bronze, 57" high. Courtesy of Bertha Schaefer Gallery, New York.

sodium carbonate. Small venting sprues from the same casting make an excellent filler rod for welding bronze castings.

The constituents of bronze often start melting out before the base metal melts and for this reason the flame must be adjusted to an excess oxygen flame to eliminate a film on the molten puddle. Careful adjustment of the oxidizing flame over a wide range will help maintain a bright surface on the metal and insure welds free from holes or gas inclusions and a balanced alloy in the weld.

Bernard Rosenthal, *Whitsuntide King,* 1960. Bronze, 63¹/₂" x 58" x 10¹/₂".
Collection of Whitney Museum of American Art, New York. Gift of Mr. &
Mrs. Samuel M. Kootz. Photo by Geoffrey Clements.

Silicon bronze has become a familiar metal for casting.
Everdur metal is perhaps the best known of the copper-silicon
alloys and welds quite easily. Generally, these alloys have
lower thermal conductivity than other bronze alloys and are
not as sensitive to overheating. During welding a liquid glass
film is formed which acts as an additional flux to protect the
molten metal. Everdur No. 26 welding rod and a silicon bronze
flux are suggested for welding Everdur.

Copper-silicon alloys contract when hot and should not be
tightly clamped. Welding should be accomplished as quickly
as possible to reduce shrinkage stress in the hot metal. When
building up a section on a casting, start at the center of the
section and complete to one edge, then return to the center of the section to complete the weld to the other edge.
This practice is also advisable whenever a previous weld is to
be heated up again by the flame.

Tom Hardy, *Fat Running Tiger*. Welded steel. "Private collection" of Mrs. Laurance Rockefeller. Courtesy of Kraushaar Galleries, New York. Photo by Colten, Inc.

Opposite
Dan Ben-Shmuel, *Large Column*, 1967. Welded copper, 48" x 53" x 112".
Courtesy of Egan Gallery, New York. Photo by Ferdinand Boesch.

WELDING COPPER — Deoxidized copper of high purity is relatively easy to weld with oxy-acetylene equipment. Working qualities, color or patina possibilities, and the availability of sheet, tubes, rods, and assorted shapes make it a desirable material for the sculptor. One of the distinct advantages of welding over soldering or brazing is that the joint or seam remains the same color and will take a patina in the same way that the base metal does. Some alloys, especially electrolytic copper, contain small amounts of oxygen or other alloying metals which make welding more difficult. A simple test of copper to determine its weldability may be made by melting a test sample. If the molten copper forms a ball or puddle which is somewhat clear and shiny, it is relatively pure and should be easy to weld. If the molten metal does not form a ball but boils and gives off quantities of fumes, impurities are indicated and the metal may be difficult to weld.

Welding techniques are much the same as those used for steel. A flux is not essential for welding pure copper but is required for most alloys. The high heat conductivity of this material requires a tip one or two sizes larger than normal. When the sculptor is working with heavy-gauge copper or on a large piece of sculpture, a pre-heating torch of air-acetylene or air-propane may be helpful to overcome the rapid transfer of heat. A modified pre-heat oven of fire brick may be quickly assembled and used to maintain a level of temperature over a large area when a sculpture is to be built up by dripping or when surface textures are being developed.

A specially prepared filler rod containing small amounts of phosphorus is recommended for welding most copper alloys. Old transformer wire, sans insulation, has proven an excellent filler material; strips of the base metal may also be used.

Oxy-Acetylene Cutting

Cutting metal by the oxy-acetylene method is accomplished by accelerating the process of oxidization — the same process which produces rust. When oxygen is united with ferrous metals at their kindling temperatures, burning results and the metal is reduced to an oxide called slag. A stream of oxygen under pressure directed at preheated steel will "burn" a hole or cut a slit through it.

A specially designed torch is necessary for most oxy-acetylene cutting operations; it is different from the regular welding blowpipe in that there are several openings in the tip and an additional lever to control the oxygen used in burning or oxidizing the metal. (An attachment which converts the welding handle for cutting is available on many models: it permits the sculptor to switch from welding operations to cutting with relative speed and ease.) A neutral flame is used in preheating the metal to kindling temperature (1400 to 1600 degrees Fahrenheit for mild carbon steel). With the torch held vertical to the surface of the metal, the pre-heating flame is applied until the metal glows bright red. At this point a stream of oxygen is introduced by depressing the pressure lever; a shower

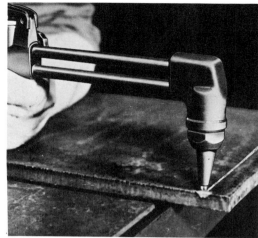

Making clean cut (step 1).

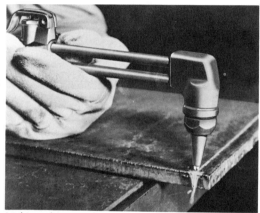

Making clean cut (step 2).

Making clean cut (step 3).

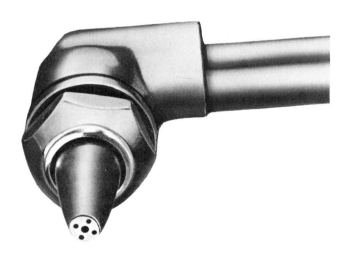

Cutting tip (nozzle). Courtesy of Union Carbide Corporation.

Photos courtesy of Union Carbide Corporation

David Annesley, *Big Ring*, 1965. Painted steel.

Tom Hardy, *Bison*. Carved steel, 55″ long. Courtesy of Kraushaar Galleries, New York. Photo by Oliver Baker Associates.

of sparks will indicate the proper burning or oxidizing of the metal. To obtain a clean cut, proper oxygen pressure (30 to 70 p.s.i.) and acetylene pressure (3 to 6 p.s.i.) must be coordinated with the correct size cutting tip for the thickness of metal to be cut. A steady, even movement of the torch along the metal will reduce the slag (oxidized metal) and size of the kerf, or channel left by the cutting torch. If the edges of the cut appear ragged and melted the torch movement is too slow; if the torch is moved too rapidly across the surface there will be insufficient pre-heat and burning or cutting of the metal will cease.

Special precautions against fire are necessary for flame-cutting operations due to the large amount of sparks or slag produced. A container of water or sand placed directly under the piece will prevent sparks from bouncing about the studio.

CUTTING PRESSURES FOR FERROUS METALS

TIP NO.	METAL THICKNESS (in.)	OXYGEN PRESSURE (p.s.i.)	ACETYLENE PRESSURE (p.s.i.) APPROX.	HAND CUTTING SPEED (in./min.)	MACHINE CUTTING SPEED (in./min.)
0	1/4	30	3	16-18	20
1	3/8	30	3	14.5-16.5	19
1	1/2	40	3	12-14.5	17
2	3/4	40	3	12-14.5	15
2	1	50	3	8.5-11.5	14
3	1-1/2	45	3	6-7.5	12
4	2	50	3	5.5-7	10
5	3	45	4	5-6.5	8
5	4	60	4	4-5	7
6	5	50	5	3.5-4.5	6
6	6	55	5	3-4	5
7	8	60	6	2.5-3.5	4
7	10	70	6	2-3	3-1/2
8	12	70	6	1.5-2	3

* Gas pressures are for hose lengths up to 25 feet. Increase pressure for longer lengths of hose.

NOTE: Acetylene pressures in above table are for tips with light preheating flames for use on clean plate. On rusty, scaly, or painted surfaces use tips with larger pre-heat flames. These tips will require higher acetylene pressures than shown above. Oxygen pressures remain the same.

Brazing

Brazing is a process of joining two pieces of metal by heating them to a temperature above 800 degrees Fahrenheit and bonding them with a non-ferrous filler metal of a lower melting point than the base metals. Brazing techniques differ from standard welding in that the base metals are not melted and fused. The joint is obtained by molecular union; the brazing metal is fused into the parent metals. Oxides or other compounds, if present, prevent the formation of properly brazed joints and for this reason flux is required. The process can be more widely applied and requires less heat than oxy-acetylene welding, and it permits the joining of two dissimilar metals. Techniques of brazing are employed by sculptors for textural effects, color, and as a protective surface for ferrous metals. Surfaces to be brazed should be cleaned thoroughly with a stiff wire brush; oil or grease may be burned off.

BRAZING TECHNIQUE — A reducing or slightly excess acetylene flame is used in most brazing operations. The outer flame zone, not the inner cone used in standard welding technique, is applied to the parent metals. A somewhat larger area is brought to a dull red heat and flux applied. Flux is used as both a cleaning agent and temperature indicator and may be applied by dipping the heated rod into the powdered flux. (Flux-coated rods are commercially available and recommended when large areas are to be brazed.) When the metal to be joined is brought to temperature the flux becomes transparent and fluid. The filler rod is touched to the metal at this time and the melted alloy will flow to the hottest point. In the standard brazing process the base metal should be sufficiently hot to melt the alloy; the flame is not applied directly to the filler rod. Excessive heat is detrimental to most brazing alloys and should be avoided. An exhaust fan or ventilation in the studio to eliminate the fumes given off during the brazing operation is a necessary safety precaution.

Sculpture in progress, Bertoia.

Edward Higgins, *Untitled*, 1964.
Welded steel and epoxy, 5' x 6½".
Courtesy of Leo Castelli Gallery, New York.
Photo by Rudolph Burckhardt.

Arc welding machine.

Arc Welding

Electric arc welding, like the oxy-acetylene process, is essentially a method of joining metals by fusing. Generally, metals heavier than ½ inch are more efficiently welded with the arc. The process is, however, more strictly limited to joining and lacks somewhat the versatility of the flame. The arc-welded joint is formed by passing electricity through a welding rod called an electrode and across a gap to the metal surfaces, producing intense heat. Molten metal from the tip of the electrode is deposited in the joint and fused with the parent metals. The gas-shielded welding processes employ an inert gas (argon or helium) to isolate the weld area and prevent atmospheric contamination. These processes (TIG and MIG) are superior for welding non-ferrous metals but require quite sophisticated equipment. They are discussed later in this chapter.

EQUIPMENT — In addition to the general equipment suggested for oxy-acetylene welding, the following items are necessary for electric arc welding:

Rectifier — Because of the limited and specialized applications of arc welding to sculpture and the relatively high cost of equipment, a combination AC/DC rectifier which can be used with metallic arc, TIG, and MIG techniques is recommended. With this type of equipment, the operator may select AC, DC straight polarity, or DC reverse polarity and thus perform all of the manual arc welding operations. In most instances, only a large studio or sculpture department will require arc equipment.

Helmet — The electric arc produces a light much more intense than that of the oxy-acetylene flame; it also gives off invisible ultraviolet and infrared rays dangerous to eyes and skin. *For this reason it is important to protect both eyes and skin with a helmet equipped with lenses specifically designed for use with the arc.*

Electrode holder — A well-designed electrode holder is essential for welding with the metallic arc. It should be reasonably light and well balanced, all exposed surfaces should be protected by insulation and remain slow to heat, and it should receive and eject electrodes easily.

Welding screen — The light from an arc is dangerous to the naked eye up to a distance of 50 feet. Whenever other people are working nearby, enclose the welding area with fire-resistant canvas or asbestos curtains. In the classroom studio, a booth may be set up to house the arc welding operation permanently.

Metal table or working surface — A metal working surface to which the ground may be attached is the most flexible arrangement. When it is not convenient to use a table a ground clamp will provide a good connection and allow the sculptor to attach directly to the piece.

SETTING UP THE EQUIPMENT — The first step in preparing the equipment is to check the cable connections to make sure they are tight. Make certain the polarity switch on the rectifier is set for the desired kind of current. Adjust the current control to the proper setting for the electrode used. This setting is approximate and should be adjusted to insure enough heat for penetration without excessive spatter and melting. A wide range of electrodes are available. Manufacturers specifications should govern the selection of the right size and kind.

Right David Jacobs, *Leaning Column*, 1965. Welded aluminum, 7½' high. Courtesy of Kornblee Gallery, New York. Photo by Eric Pollitzer.

Anthony Caro, *Midday*, 1960. Painted steel, 94" x 38" x 150". Collection of Timothy and Paul Caro. Courtesy of Andre Emmerich Gallery, New York.

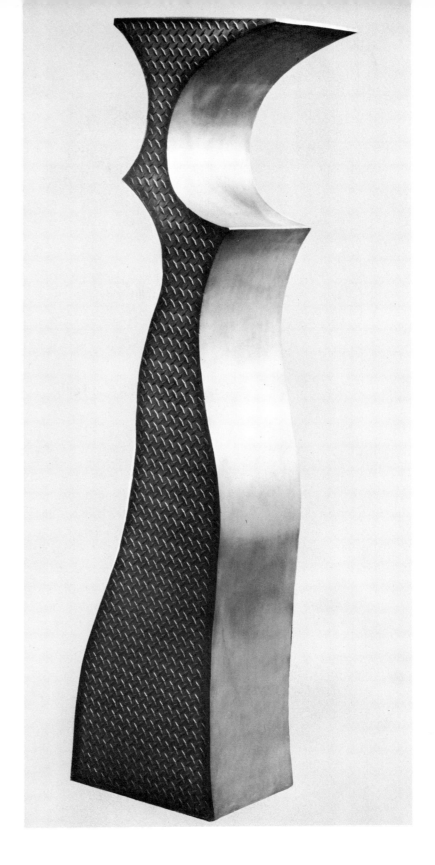

Striking the Arc: A basic operation in preparing for arc welding is striking an arc to establish a current flow across an open space between the electrode and base metal. A tapping or scratching motion is used to make contact and the electrode is immediately withdrawn to a distance equal to the diameter of the rod. If the electrode is allowed to remain in contact with the base metal, it will stick and become red hot. *If the electrode does weld to the base metal, break it loose by twisting or bending; if it cannot be broken loose quickly, disengage the holder.*

BASIC TECHNIQUE — The arc which spans the gap between electrode and joint generates heat sufficient to melt the edges of the base metal and electrode filler. A spark gap approximately the diameter of the electrode should be maintained to form a pool or puddle of molten metal. The electrode is held in a near-vertical position and moved just rapidly enough to insure fusion with the base metals. If the current is properly set and the arc maintained at an even length, a characteristic crackling sound will result. Two important factors are correct current and arc length. If the current is too high, excessive heat is generated and melting of the base metals results; if too low, there is insufficient heat to form a molten pool. When the arc is too long, it wanders and the arc stream dissipates, causing considerable spatter and poor control; too short an arc reduces penetration and the filler builds up on the surface.

Tungsten Inert-Gas Welding (TIG)

The TIG welding process involves striking an arc from a tungsten electrode in an inert-gas (argon or helium) shielded atmosphere and fusing the base metals and filler in a manner similar to oxy-acetylene welding. The process has been called TIG (Tungsten Inert Gas), Tungsten arc welding, Heliarc, and Heliweld. A tungsten electrode is mounted in a gas shielding cup (ceramic or water-cooled) which directs the flow of gas to the weld area. Argon is heavier and diffuses more easily than helium and requires considerably less volume. It is more readily available from welding suppliers and thus recommended.

EQUIPMENT — (A DC reverse-polarity system or high-frequency stabilization on AC is used). In addition to the AC/DC rectifier already mentioned above, the following are necessary for the inert gas welding process:

Torch — A good torch should consist of an insulated handle, porcelain or water-cooled cup, tungsten electrode and a combination cable designed to carry electricity, inert gas, and water.

Tanks — One steel cylinder of argon (or helium), leased or rented from supplier.

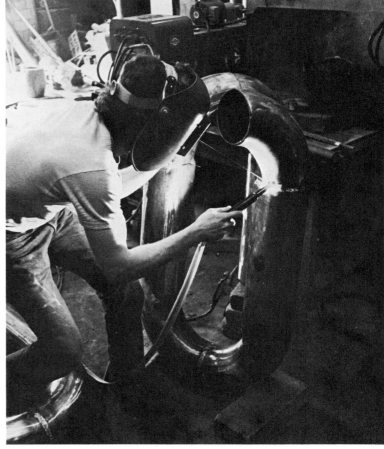

Sculptor Stanley Mock welding cast bronze sections using TIG process.

Pressure regulator — Similar to oxygen equipment, the argon regulator should have one tank gauge and one line-pressure gauge.

Flow meter and circulating water pump — These are required if the tungsten torch is cooled by circulating water (the water passes through the torch at rates varying between 10 and 25 gallons per hour). A water-pressure gauge and water strainer are additional helpful accessories for water-cooled equipment.

WELDING TECHNIQUE — The technique of TIG welding is in many ways similar to gas welding. The non-consumable tungsten electrode is held at an approximate 85-degree angle and moved opposite the tilt angle with a steady even motion. Strike the arc by holding the electrode horizontally over the work (AC with high-frequency stabilization) or by touching the work (if DC is used) and withdrawing to approximately 1/8 inch above the metal. Develop a puddle at the beginning of the weld and insert the filler rod into it. The filler rod should be held at quite a flat angle (approximately 10 to 20 degrees). The torch movement should be forward with a slight hesitation and forward again across the width of the molten puddle to form the ripples characteristic of this technique.

Welding metal sections using MIG process. Photo by J. Falkoner.

Metallic Inert-Gas Welding (MIG)

Like TIG, the MIG welding process employs a shield of inert gas to protect the weld area. Unlike TIG however, this process uses a continuous consumable wire electrode which is fed through the torch at preset speeds. Molten metal from the wire electrode is deposited in the joint to be welded and fused with the parent metals. The hand-held welding gun delivers current, shielding gas, and wire to the weld area and is either air or water cooled.

The MIG process has many advantages and is the preferred method of many sculptors for welding both ferrous and non-ferrous metals of any thickness. (Until recently TIG was considered best for welding thin sheet because of its lower current; however, the development of a short circuiting transfer technique for MIG is equally adaptable to use with thin stock.) While the original investment in TIG or MIG equipment is considerable, the following advantages should be considered for large production or studio situations:

1. Faster welding, since starting and stopping to replace electrodes, as with metallic arc stick welding, is eliminated. Also, weld failures due to stopping, such as cold lapping, cracking, or slag inclusions, are greatly reduced due to the continuous feed of the metal electrode.

2. Deep penetration; the size of fillet welds may be reduced and small bevels on joints are possible. (A fillet weld is a weld applied to a joint where one plate is placed perpendicular to another.)

3. Clean welds; because there is no slag or flux to remove and very little spatter, considerable saving in clean-up time may be realized. Corrosive fluxes on aluminum may be eliminated entirely.

4. Ease of welding; when equipment is properly set, all the welder needs to do is to press the trigger and weld. His main concern is to watch the angle of the welding gun and travel speed. A few hours is usually all that is required to become proficient at the technique of MIG welding.

Non-Ferrous Metals and Alloys

5

Before he becomes involved in one of the various casting processes, the sculptor-founder must decide whether to compound his own alloy or select from a large number of alloys used in industry. He therefore needs to understand some of the methods used in extracting or reducing metals other than iron from their ores. He must also be aware of how they are refined for specific applications and must be familiar with the qualities and properties of these metals.

Non-ferrous metals are those which contain no iron and as a result have no magnetic attraction. A simple test with a magnet will determine iron content in a metal of unknown alloy. The non-ferrous metals are often classified in two groups: the pure metals (primary or base metals for alloys), and those which are used chiefly as alloying agents. The classification is not altogether adequate since all of the metals in the primary group are important alloying agents and many in the other group are used as base metals.

Few metals are found in their pure state in nature. It is understandable that the three most important ones, copper, gold, and silver, were extensively used by early civilizations. Copper, lead, zinc, nickel, and antimony are usually obtained from sulfide ores; metals such as tin and aluminum are obtained principally from oxide ores.

The earliest and still most common method of extracting metals from their ores is by a fusion process involving the following steps:

1. That part of the ore containing the mineral is concentrated by removing rock, earth, and other materials. Tedious

BASE METALS	
Aluminum	Nickel
Copper	Platinum
Gold	Silver
Lead	Tin
Magnesium	Zinc

ALLOYING AGENTS

Antimony
Arsenic
Beryllium

NON-METAL ALLOYING AGENTS

Carbon	Phosphorus
Nitrogen	Silicon
Oxygen	Sulfur

Opposite
Sculpture Foundry, the Art Institute of Chicago. Photo by J. Falkoner.

early methods of hand picking the ore pile have been replaced in current times by mechanical processes. Water-washed gravity methods are the most common. Crushed ore is washed on an inclined surface; short rapid rotation of the washing table causes the heavier particles containing mineral to flow off the lower edge of the table. Rock, earth, and other lighter particles are delivered to another position on the washing table.

A second common method of concentrating mineral ores is by flotation, essentially the reverse of gravity washing. The ore is ground to a size comparable to sand, flooded with water, and chemicals added to form a film over the mineral content. Compressed air is released into the tank agitating the mix. The minerals, covered by film, adhere to air bubbles and are carried to an overflow outlet at the top of the tank. The waste materials, rock and earth, do not become coated and remain at the bottom of the tank, where they are drawn off. This process effectively concentrates the ores of one metal but may also be used to separate the ores of combination metals from one another by adjusting the filming chemicals.

2. Sulfide ores are roasted to remove most of the sulfur content; this in effect changes the sulfide ore to oxides, which may be reduced to metal later. Air currents are passed over the heated sulfide ore furnishing the oxygen necessary to the process. The metal oxide remains as a solid while the sulfur dioxide gas passes off. A variation of the heating or roasting process calls for closely controlled temperature (approximately 900 to 1000 degrees Fahrenheit) and limited air supply, to form the sulfate rather than the oxide. This variation is often desirable if the ore is to be leached or processed by chemicals to remove the metal.

3. Concentrated ores are next subjected to a smelting oper-

ation to obtain the metal. The process involves heating the oxidized ore to a high temperature with coke or charcoal, which pulls oxygen from the metal. The metal is then free to form a molten mass under the lighter oxides. In order to ensure complete separation of the metal from the somewhat infusible oxides, flux is added to create a fluid mixture called slag, which floats on top of the metal. Common fluxes used in the smelting operation are limestone, sand, fluorspar, and soda salts. Crude metal is formed as a result of the smelting operation with the majority of non-ferrous metals. In some instances, however — as with copper and nickel — the first smelting operation produces a fused sulfide called a matte. Additional operations are necessary to produce metal from the matte. Aluminum and other metals which may be easily oxidized are reduced by electrolysis of a fused salt rather than by smelting.

After the smelting operation crude metal is given a refining treatment to remove impurities and to separate metals which may be combined. There are a large number of refining operations possible to prepare non-ferrous metals for use. Four of the most basic methods include:

1. Refining by fire — accomplished by remelting the metal, oxidizing the impurities and removing them;
2. Refining by chemical — impurities are dissolved through the use of chemical reagents;
3. Refining by electrolysis — the electrolytic deposition of a pure metal which leaves impurities undissolved in the electrolyte;
4. Refining by distillation — limited to those metals which can be volatilized and recondensed within a workable temperature range.

Some metals require the application of two or more of the above procedures to complete refining; other minor metals are produced only as a by-product of such refining operations.

Alloying is the process of combining a number of pure metals to produce unique and useful properties in non-ferrous materials. In a small melt in a studio foundry, the base charge may have high percentage of scrap or none at all. The charge is melted down with precautions to prevent contamination from fuel or atmosphere. Additions for alloying that are not easily oxidized may be melted with the charge, while those additions which have a high rate of attraction for oxygen are added just prior to pouring. With some alloys, small additions such as phos-copper are necessary to remove certain gases from the melt or to overcome impurities. The most common results of alloying are to increase strength and hardness, but changes in the metal may also include special results such as increasing ductility, corrosion resistance, and change of color.

There are a large number of non-ferrous alloys commercially available, and it is often difficult for the sculptor to choose the one that is exactly suited to his special applications and foundry capability. Even slight differences in foundry conditions can make large differences in the behavior of an alloy. Tradition and experience are not always the best guides in choosing an alloy nor in helping the artist determine whether or not to compound his own. The standard properties of strength and ductility are usually first considerations and there are many alloys that will measure up to these requirements, but there may be only one or two alloys which will meet color requirements or special problems of corrosion resistance.

Copper-Base Alloys

BRASS — The best known and most widely used of all non-ferrous alloys are the copper-zinc combinations known as brasses. Brasses have outstanding working qualities, good strength and high corrosion resistance. Compositions in the binary alloys of copper and zinc range from approximately 99% copper down to about 55% copper. With a low percentage of zinc (under 10%) the alloy remains essentially the same color as copper; between 10% and 15% it changes to a bronze color. Gold color is achieved when the zinc content reaches 15% to 20% zinc and the familiar yellow brass color is present when zinc content is between 20% and 40%; above 40% the alloys appear reddish.

As the zinc content of brass is increased up to about 40% there is an increase in the tensile strength. Brasses containing up to 39% zinc are classified alpha brasses because of the single constituent alpha solid solution. Above 39% zinc a second constituent is present, beta solid solution. Such brasses are known as beta brasses or Muntz metal.

An induction furnace is used to melt most brasses and melting is accomplished as rapidly as possible to prevent the loss of zinc. A cover is not normally necessary but charcoal may be used to prevent oxidation. The temperature for pour is usually several hundred degrees above melt. Pouring temperature and rate of pour need to be much more carefully controlled than with other non-ferrous combinations.

Muntz Metal. This alloy (60% copper; 41% zinc) is extremely plastic at bright red heat and lends itself readily to forging and stretching operations. It can be cold worked to increase its tensile strength and hardness. Extensive cold working requires that the metal be annealed between workings.

Cartridge Brass. Also called 70:30 or spinning brass, this alloy (70% copper; 30% zinc) has been employed extensively for making shells, from which is derived its name. It has excellent working properties and is used for many spinning and drawing operations.

BRONZE — Copper-tin alloys are known as bronzes. There are very few modern bronzes which are straight copper-tin combinations. Most bronzes used today contain several other elements including zinc, aluminum, nickel, manganese and phosphorus. The tin content in bronze alloys seldom exceeds 10% although in ancient times bronze containing 16% tin was very important. The ancients discovered that rapid cooling or quenching of the hot metal produced a soft, easily worked material while slow cooling produced a hard metal.

For most foundry operations bronze is melted in a crucible.

ngots may be melted under a charcoal covering, but usually the best results are obtained by combining the raw materials in the melting process. The copper is melted first; if the copper appears wild as it melts, manganese (carbon free) is added (approximately 1 ounce of manganese to 100 pounds of copper). Alloying metals, usually zinc and tin, are then added. Phosphorus (phos-copper in the form of shot) may be added as a deoxidizer near the end of the melt. Melting and pouring temperatures should be kept as low as feasible for the particular casting to reduce excessive zinc volatilization and tin oxidation. High temperatures may also produce a coarse, weak, crystalline structure. Pouring normally takes place between 1950 and 2300 degrees Fahrenheit.

Admiralty Metal. Used extensively in sea-going vessels, this alloy (70% copper; 29% zinc; 1% tin) has high corrosion resistance, good strength and ductility. Variations of admiralty include: Tobin bronze (60% copper; 38% zinc; 2% tin) and manganese bronze (58% copper; 37% zinc; 3% ferro manganese; 2% iron).

Phosphor bronze. Most copper tin alloys used today contain small amounts of phosphorus. Phosphorus is used as a deoxidizer and even those alloys with only a trace are known as phosphor bronze. Tin content varies from 1% to 10%. Lead is often added to approximately 5% to produce a metal more suitable to chasing and working the finished casting.

Silicon bronze. Silicon bronze combines the strength of mild steel with the corrosion resistance of copper alloys. Most silicon alloys contain about 95% copper, 3% silicon, and various percentages of elements such as manganese, tin, zinc, or aluminum. Trade names for silicon bronzes include: Everdur, Herculoy, Duronze, and Olympic Bronze. The relative ease by which the silicon bronzes may be melted and the limited need for flux or charcoal cover make it a desirable alloy for use in a small foundry.

Aluminum Silicon. The aluminum silicon combinations have exceptional casting characteristics coupled with high corrosion resistance. These alloys are highly desirable for intricate configurations. The most common alloy in this group is called 43 which contains 5% of silicon and has excellent casting qualities. The aluminum silicon alloys up to 12% silicon are exceptionally strong but must be treated in the molten condition with a sodium or potassium compound to obtain the best casting properties. Such treatment is known as modification.

Aluminum Bronze. Aluminum bronzes are copper alloys containing between 4% and 10% of aluminum; in addition many compositions contain such alloying elements as iron, nickel, and manganese. The most common of these alloys contain 88% copper, 9% aluminum, 3% iron or 95% copper, and 5% aluminum.

In some of the non-ferrous alloys, compounds in solution are much harder than individual metals. Such compounds do not stay permanently in solution in some alloys, but precipitate as individual particles dispersed throughout the material by aging or, in some instances, with heat treatment. This change in the structure of the metal alloy is called age hardening. The age-hardening aluminum bronze generally contains 10% or more aluminum.

Other Age-Hardening Alloys. A number of copper alloys are age hardenable. An alloy containing 85% copper, 8% tin, and 7% nickel is an excellent age-hardening alloy. A commercial material known as Tempaloy is such an alloy.

Beryllium bronze or Beryllium copper shows exceptional strength on aging. With between 2% and 3% beryllium remarkable strength is achieved for a non-ferrous material. Non-sparking wrenches for use with oxy-acetylene welding equipment are often made from these alloys.

Traditional Bronze Alloys. The ancient alloy which is perhaps still the most widely used in traditional foundries is known as 85-5-5-5. Sometimes called ounce metal or red brass it contains 85% copper, 5% tin, 5% zinc, and 5% lead. A variation which is also used extensively calls for 89% copper, 6% tin, 2% lead, 3% zinc. These are the alloys most commonly used by sculptor-founders who wish to compound their own alloy in a studio foundry. Variations which exclude lead are called gun metal or Government bronze.

Cupro Nickel Alloys. The copper-nickel combinations contain up to 30% nickel, which effectively changes the characteristic copper color. The color in these alloys becomes lighter with increasing nickel content until with 25% nickel the alloy is entirely white. Coinage metal is usually 75% copper and 25% nickel. Cupro nickel alloys containing more than 20% nickel have extremely high corrosion resistance and are excellent for fountains and other high corrosive conditions where a white color is desirable.

Alik Cavalierre, *Three x Three x Three*, 1962. Bronze. Courtesy of Martha Jackson Gallery, New York.

Aluminum

Bauxite is the hydrated oxide used in the production of aluminum. The ore usually contains impurities such as oxides of iron, silicon, and titanium which must be removed before the ore can be electrically treated to remove the aluminum. The mineral cryolite is a necessary constituent of the electrolytic bath used in aluminum production. Bauxite must be refined to yield a high-purity aluminum; the oxides of iron, silicon, or titanium usually present with aluminum oxide are reduced in the electrolytic bath and remain in the electrolyte. The first step in obtaining a pure aluminum oxide is accomplished chemically by dissolving the ore with caustic soda to form sodium aluminate. The aluminum is then precipitated as the hydroxide by decomposition of the sodium aluminate. When heated the hydroxide breaks down to the pure aluminum oxide.

The first process for the electrolytic reduction of aluminum was developed by two men working independently — one in the United States, another in France — and is known as the Hall-Heroult process. It is based on the phenomenon that aluminum oxide will dissolve in a bath of molten cryolite from which the aluminum may then be electrolyzed. A large, round-bottomed container is used; the inside lining of the container is carbon, which carries the negative charge and acts as the cathode of the cell. The molten bath of cryolite containing 25% aluminum oxide is kept at approximately 1800 degrees Fahrenheit by electrical current. The anode or positive charge consists of carbon bars suspended in the bath. The current passing through the tank causes molten aluminum to be deposited on the bottom of the tank, where it is drawn off.

In most industrial foundries aluminum and its alloys are melted in iron crucibles lined with a lime wash. Aluminum may also be melted in a graphite foundry crucible. The melt progresses slowly to prevent overheating, which results in a coarse-grain structure in the casting and excessive oxidation of the molten metal. Melt temperature varies between 1250 and 1350 degress Fahrenheit. Normally, fluxes are not used to melt aluminum, but a mixture of aluminum chloride and zinc chloride acts as an effective flux in some cases. Industry often uses a chlorine gas atmosphere to protect molten aluminum, but it is dangerous and not generally feasible in a small foundry.

ALLOYING ALUMINUM — Most of the elements used to develop an alloy of aluminum have higher melting points than the base metals and as a result must be added in a pre-alloyed state. Such additions for alloying aluminum are called hardeners. Hardeners are available commercially; the silicon hardener contains 70% aluminum and 30% silicon; copper hardener is 50% aluminum, 50% copper; sometimes manganese and nickel are introduced, not to exceed 10% each. Most hardeners are brittle and may be broken up and added to the molten aluminum or melted separately and added to the melt.

MELTING POINTS OF METALS

METAL	TEMPERATURE (°F.)
Aluminum	1220
Brass	1650
Aluminum bronze	1645
Phosphor bronze 5 %	1920
Silicon bronze	1865
Copper	1980
Gold	1945
Lead	620
Muntz metal	1660
Sterling silver	1760
Tin	449
Zinc	786

Casting—Lost Wax

6

The *cire-perdue* or lost wax process is the best known and most widely used of the traditional methods for casting metal sculpture. Variations of the process were known to many ancient civilizations. The Chinese cast bronze statuary and ceremonial vessels in this manner before 4000 B.C. Early Greeks employed the process to cast their monumental bronzes. Larger pieces were often cast in sections and later joined by highly sophisticated soldering or riveting techniques. The sculptors of West Africa, at Benin and Ife, cast portrait heads of exceptional quality over cores of fire clay and manure. Masters of the Renaissance used "lost wax" extensively; the sculptor sometimes cast the piece in his own studio, as Cellini did with his *Perseus,* but more often he employed the services of a foundry to reproduce the final bronze from a clay or plaster model.

This tradition of foundry production of bronze sculpture, prevailing since the Renaissance, has tended to separate the art of the sculptor and the craft of the founder. A model was prepared in clay or plaster by the sculptor then transported to the foundry, there to be cast in metal by highly skilled artisans. A good foundry was vital to the production of cast sculpture. Rodin's founder Rudier became world-famous because of his ability to reproduce, with exceptional fidelity, the minute detail, nature, and character of the model.

Foundries which specialize in casting sculpture follow elaborate procedures, often dictated more by tradition than efficiency, to reproduce in bronze an exact replica of the sculptor's clay or plaster model. The processes are time-consuming and very costly. The following is a brief description of one such method.

Male head and female head, Kingdom of Benin. Courtesy of The University Museum, University of Pennsylvania.

Opposite
Benvenuto Cellini, *Perseus*. Bronze.

A gelatine sectional mold backed by a plaster shell is made from the sculptor's clay or plaster pattern. This reproduces in fine detail the surface of the model. The shell is removed in sections and layers of wax are painted on the inside surfaces of the gelatine mold to a thickness of approximately $1/8$ to $1/4$ inch. The wax coating will eventually be replaced by bronze. Its thickness, therefore, is determined by the size of the piece and the amount of strength required for support. When the wax is cool and firm, the gelatine mold is removed; detailing or retouching will bring the wax replica to its finished state. Sprues and gates in the form of wax rods are then attached to the wax. These rods will provide openings in the mold through which the bronze will eventually be poured and gasses allowed to escape. Investment material which will form the mold is then poured in and around the hollow wax shell; iron or steel core pins are placed through the wax and embedded in investment on both sides, preventing the core from shifting once the wax is burned out. The invested wax is then placed in a kiln to burn out the wax and thoroughly dry the investment material. The heated mold containing the negative cavity is packed in sand, usually in a specially prepared pit in the foundry floor. Molten bronze is poured from a crucible into the main opening or pouring funnel of the mold, filling the cavity. Vents allow air and gasses to escape. After pouring, the metal is allowed to cool slowly, the investment is broken away, sprues and gates are

Above
Bronze sacrificial wine holder with stand, China (early Chon). Courtesy of The University Museum, University of Pennsylvania.

Right
Joseph Konzal, *Three Cities*, 1966 (Project B). Firebrick (carving for bronze), $15^1/2''$ high. Courtesy of Bertha Schaefer Gallery, New York.

Right
Henry Moore, *Lincoln Center Reclining Figure*, 1965. Bronze, 16' x 30'. Gift of Albert A. List Foundation. Courtesy of Lincoln Center for the Performing Arts. Photo by Ezra Stoller.

Joseph Konzal, *Sparta*, 1966 (Three cities project). Wood for bronze, 20" high, and bronze, 24" high. Courtesy of Bertha Schaefer Gallery, New York.

removed, and the piece is chased, cleaned, and finished.

Contemporary sculptor-founders working in their own studio foundries have developed many variations of the traditional *cire-perdue* process. Most often, they choose to work directly in wax, thereby eliminating cumbersome techniques of reproducing a wax from a plaster mold. The pattern for sculpture may be built up over a pre-cast core, developed from sheet, or carved out of solid wax. It may incorporate other materials: wood, paper, straw, styrofoam, or almost any material that can be burned out of the mold leaving little or no residue.

Significant factors leading to the development of studio foundries are the cost and time needed to reproduce a cast in commercial foundries. Of even greater importance to many sculptors is the direct control of each process employed to shape his finished work. In his own foundry, he is able to respond to the metal of the final form with a sensitivity and understanding possible only through such direct involvement.

Numerous wax formulas, both natural and synthetic, have been developed to meet the exacting requirements of industry and technology. Perhaps the most sophisticated techniques and materials have been developed by dental technicians and manufacturers of precision instruments. Such developments have made available inexpensive waxes with a wide variety of properties suitable for use in bronze casting.

Properties of Wax

BURN-OUT — One of the prime considerations in choosing a wax for the lost wax process is that it be removable by heat without leaving a residue in the mold caviety. Ash, soot, or resinous waste left in the investment could contaminate the final casting. Complete burn-out of the wax should occur between 800 and 1000 degrees Fahrenheit:

STRENGTH — The ability of the wax to retain the intended shape through the pattern forming and investing procedures is also an important requirement. A wax that is soft may be distorted by the weight of investment material and require props or added support. When modeling directly in wax, it is sometimes difficult to realize all of the possibilities of strength and tension inherent in the cast metal. A large piece of sculpture which is balanced on a thin supporting shaft might be quite easily achieved in bronze but difficult to construct in wax. Several waxes with varying degrees of hardness may be used on one model or the wax may be reinforced with wood or straw for support.

ECONOMY — As the name of the process implies, the wax will be lost or burned out and in most instances not available for re-use. Economy and ease of preparation are, therefore, factors for consideration.

DUCTILITY — Certain applications will require different working properties. For modeling, the wax should be somewhat soft and pliable with a wide working temperature range. For dipping, pouring, or brushing, a wax with low viscosity is desirable, so that a coating over a core or in a mold may be rapidly built.

Microcrystalline wax is widely used in bronze casting today. It is relatively inexpensive, readily available and requires little or no preparation for use. It is a synthetic wax, a by-product of the petroleum industry. The name is derived from a crystalline structure smaller than that of paraffin or natural waxes. The microcrystalline waxes are more pliable over a wider range of temperature than are natural waxes and often have higher melting points. In addition, they burn out completely under 900 degrees Fahrenheit and leave no residue. They possess many qualities which the sculptor finds desirable — toughness, pliability, and good fusion — both with and without the application of heat.

Working the Wax

Modeling wax may be melted in a double boiler or be kept soft and pliable floating in warm water. Microcrystalline wax does not take water from the air and will bond or laminate to itself wet or dry. Sheets of wax for modeling or construction may be formed in desired thickness by pouring melted wax onto wet plaster or marble slabs. A simple two-piece plaster mold to cast wax rods for gates and sprues may be made using lengths of wood dowel from 1/4-inch diameter to 1-inch diameter as models. Small sprues are made by rolling the wax out on a flat surface with the palm of the hand. Many sculptors who model in wax find that when a quantity of wax is placed in a shirt pocket or inside an apron, body heat keeps it just warm enough to work easily. A simple heating unit for softening wax may be constructed using a light bulb in a small closed box.

Tools for modeling wax are made from the harder fruitwoods, rosewood, or lignum vitae, and treated with oils or melted wax to prevent their sticking to the model. Metal tools range from old knives to dental instruments. Padding and insulating the handles permits metal tools to be heated over a hot plate or alcohol lamp. Soldering irons make excellent tools for working wax patterns. An instant-heat soldering gun with a flat broad tip (approximately 1/2 square inch) is an excellent wax modeling instrument.

The thickness of forms for casting should be carefully regulated. Some small bronzes may be cast solid, but generally 1/2 inch is the maximum desirable casting thickness. A thickness of between 1/8 and 1/4 inch is satisfactory for most purposes. Protrusions, corners, and points of attachment to a base require additional thickness.

A direct approach which may be used to achieve a basic form for casting involves building, carving, or modeling a mixture of plaster and silica sand. This form is a core to which wax is then applied by dipping or painting and modeling. The wax pattern for sculpture is in this way built up and completed over the core; core pins are inserted, sprues are attached, and it is ready for investing.

A similar process for large, massive forms involves adding a short, wide gate and vents to the solid wax piece. The model is covered with a coating of investment material to a thickness of approximately 2 inches and allowed to set up before the piece with its casing is placed in an oven at a temperature 30 or 40 degrees above the melting point of the wax. When all of the wax has been drained from the cavity (it may be retained for future use) and the casing cooled, a shell of wax is then built up on the inner surface. If the form is open at the base, or the gate wide enough, the wax shell may be developed by painting. If it is not feasible to use a brush, a process similar to ceramic-slush casting may be employed. In this case, melted wax is poured into the cavity and allowed to solidify against the cool inner surface; when the desired thickness is achieved, the still-liquid excess wax is poured off. Core pins are added (it may be necessary to drill pilot holes to prevent splitting the set casing), the core poured, and the unit invested. The gate and venting systems are extensions of the ones used to pour the wax shell.

Sculptor Jack Mays modeling directly in wax.

WAX FORMULAS

MODELING - 1		MODELING - 2		CARVING, DIPPING, PAINTING	
Beeswax	50%	Beeswax	40%	Beeswax	20%
Paraffin	40%	Paraffin	40%	Paraffin	30%
Petroleum jelly	7%	Rosin	15%	Ceresin	30%
Lanolin	3%	Petroleum jelly	5%	Carnauba	20%

Microcrystalline wax is a widely used synthetic (petroleum derivative). It is inexpensive and is adaptable for carving, dipping, and modeling (170 Amber 172°F.).

MODELING WAXES

WAX	SOURCE	MELTING RANGE (°F.)	SOLUBLE	REMARKS
Beeswax	natural honeycomb of bee	144 - 147	alcohol acetone	Foundation of traditional wax formulas. Too hard and brittle to be worked by itself.
Ceresin	earth wax ozocerite	145 - 180	hot oil alcohol benzene	Tough, little shrinkage, brittle by itself.
Carnauba		180 - 190	alcohol turpentine hot oil	Adds strength to wax formulas. High shrinkage.
Tallow	animal fat		hot oils	Costly; perishable. Adds plasticity and softens formulas.
Microcrystalline	petroleum derivative	From 145 to above 300; 40 or more grades.	alcohol oil turpentine	Most suitable for sculpture as is. Many varieties to choose from.
Paraffin	petroleum derivative	120 - 145	alcohol turpentine olive oil	Used to thin a formula, reduce stickiness, improve carving qualities.

WAX ADDITIVES

MATERIAL	SOURCE		SOLUBLE	REMARKS
Rosin	turpentine distillation		Methyl alcohol	Lowers melting point of wax formula. Increases malleability of formula. May increase stickiness. Rosin may be toughened by addition of 15 % glycerin.
Lanolin	sheep wool		Ether	Softens wax formula. Increases plasticity. Of special value in cold weather.
Petroleum jelly	petroleum derivative			Softens wax formula.
Mineral oil	mineral			Softens wax formula.

Sprue System

A sprue system is the network of wax rods attached to the model and connecting it with the pouring funnel. The sprues, which are put in place just prior to investment, perform three major functions in the casting process. They form the openings through which the melted wax of the pattern may run off in the initial stages of the burn-out procedure. The main channels, or runners, of this system permit molten metal to be introduced and fed to all parts of the mold cavity. A group of smaller openings permit the escape of gas generated by the molten metal during pouring and air that might otherwise be trapped inside the mold.

The major elements of the sprue system are identified as follows: *Sprue* is often used as a general term for all passages of the system. It is also used to identify the main runners which receive molten metal from the pouring funnel. The *pouring funnel* is the largest external opening in the mold. It receives the molten metal directly from the crucible and acts as a reservoir to insure steady and even entrance into the runners of the system. *Runners* are the main feeder channels which carry the metal from the pouring funnel to the pattern cavity. A *gate* is the point where the runner is attached to the model. The pouring funnel is often referred to as the "pouring gate." The channel through which the melted wax of the model escapes during the burn-out procedure in upright and draft systems is called the *drain*. *Risers* are vents which allow for the escape of air or gas which otherwise might be trapped in the mold cavity.

SPRUE DESIGN — Each wax model for sculpture requires a uniquely tailored sprue arrangement. Size, complexity of shape, and consistency of thickness must be carefully considered when determining the number of runners and risers and their placement. Each large section usually requires its own runner to insure a gradual and unified solidification of metal. The metal of the casting itself should be the first to solidify, with progressive solidification proceeding from the center of the mold outward to the pouring funnel. The entire sprue system will need to be removed after divesting; therefore, gates and

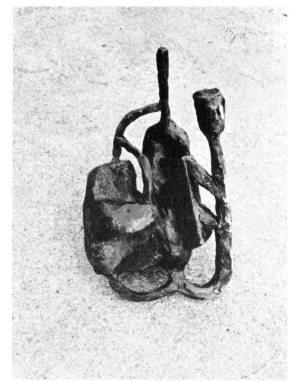

Sculpture with sprue system attached.

Sprue system

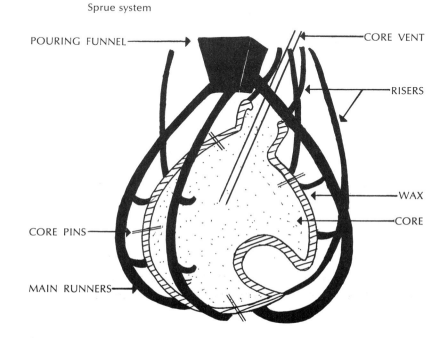

POURING FUNNEL

CORE VENT

RISERS

WAX

CORE

CORE PINS

MAIN RUNNERS

93

risers should be placed to allow for easy removal and cleanup. Wherever possible, the point of attachment to the model should be a high or convex surface.

SPRUE SIZE AND SHAPE — The heavy sprues and runners of the system should normally be as short as possible. Molten metal will tend to solidify as it comes in contact with the inner mold surface. For this reason, the length of the runner is directly relative to its diameter — the longer the runner the larger its diameter must be to prevent solidification of the runner before the cavity is filled. The minimum diameter of runners should be approximately one and one-half times the thickness of the area being fed, both to insure complete filling and to reduce porosity at the gate. Heavy feeder sprues in complex sprue systems would range from four to six times the thickness of the model. Risers are generally smaller in diameter than the wall thickness. The pouring funnel acts as a reservoir for the metal entering the runners of the system and should therefore be large enough to insure continual flow at least equal to the total of the diameter of all runners of the system. A square or pyramid-shaped pouring funnel will prevent swirling of the molten metal and entrapment of air as it enters the mold cavity.

Investment

The wax model with its sprue system complete is ready to be invested or encased in a refractory compound which makes a mold for casting. (The invested wax or other materials of the model will be eliminated or burned out to be replaced with molten metal.) A good investment material will retain with fidelity the impression of the model, withstand the changes of temperature to which it is exposed, contain and support molten metal poured into it, and provide the requisite degree of porosity for the escape of gas. Many kinds of investment material have been used in the *cire-perdue* process.

Some compounds developed for industry or dental casting techniques meet rigid requirements for close tolerance control. Primitive founders have used natural materials such as earth, clay, manure, ash, and sand with excellent results.

The selection of an appropriate investment material will be determined by factors of economy, weight, and availability of materials, coupled with the unique requirements of the foundry and configuration of the piece to be cast. The most widely used compound in studio foundries consists of a binder — usually a high quality molding plaster which provides the necessary strength in the mold, and a refractory — silica sand, grog (ground up brick or fired ceramic), fire clay, or luto (old used investment which has been reprocessed) to increase the porosity necessary for the release of moisture during burn-out and escape of gas during the pouring operation, (formulas are given later in this chapter).

MIXING — Ingredients of the investment formula are first dry-mixed to insure even consistency. The mixture is then sifted into water to make a heavy paste. Small quantities of a thicker mixture are used when it is to be applied to the model by brush or spatula. For pouring the backing or entire mold, the investment should be mixed and allowed to partially set until ready to pour. Pouring readiness may be determined by running the fingers across the surface of the wet plaster investment. When the furrows created by the fingers remain distinct, it is ready. Heavier refractory materials will have a tendency to sink to the bottom of the mixture and must be kept in solution by constant mixing. The mixing of plaster compounds should be accomplished with as little disturbance of the surface as possible to avoid the entrapment of air. One method commonly used is to extend the arm into the compound and stir with the fingers. Tapping or vibrating the mixing container will assist the removal of air bubbles from the mix.

POURING INVESTMENT — Pouring of investment should be continuous, to prevent a split or separation in the mold. When it is not possible to complete an investment in one pour, scouring or roughening the surface of the partial fill will assist the adhesion of material subsequently added. A surface-tension reducer may be used on the surface of a wax model to prevent the formation of air bubbles. Alcohol and thin solu-

tions of soap and water have been used with some success; more efficient debubbleizers are commercially available from dental supply houses.

The pattern to be invested is placed in a flask or container which will hold the investment until it is set. Once the mold sets up, the flask or container is stripped away and ready for burn-out. A steel mesh of 14 to 16 gauge wire makes an excellent reinforcement for the mold exterior. Handles may be attached to this wire for ease in moving heavy investments. The wire mesh is made into a round or oval cylinder, and heavy brown paper is secured to the outside to contain the liquid investment. The model, in wax or with a surface coating of investment, is centered in the container. A minimum of 2 inches clearance is recommended for the mold wall and 3 inches at the base. For thicker castings and heavy sprue systems, increased wall and base thicknesses are desirable to resist the weight of descending metal. The pattern may be placed on a block of pre-cast investment or suspended inside the flask to insure adequate mold thickness at the base.

The following are fine investment mixes for the reproduction of minute surface and textural detail:

1. asbestos shorts — 1 part
   molding plaster — 2 parts
   flint — 2 parts
2. grog (ceramic) 100 mesh — 1 part
   luto 100 mesh — 1 part
   plaster — 1 part

General mixes for the body of the mold are:

1. silica sand — 3 parts
   molding plaster — 1 part
2. silica sand — 1 part
   luto — 1 part
   molding plaster — 1 part
3. silica sand — 1 part
   molding plaster — 1 part
   luto — 2 parts

For large molds to reduce weight, use:

1. molding plaster — 1 part
   luto — 1 part
   mica (Perlite) — 1 part
   silica sand — 1 part
2. molding plaster — 1 part
   mica — 3 parts
   silica sand — 1 part

Invested wax being loaded in kiln for burnout.

Burn-out

The procedure by which the wax model invested in a mold is prepared to receive molten metal for the final cast is called burn-out. The purposes of burn-out are to eliminate the model completely, leaving no ash or residue, and to drive off all moisture (curing the mold and thus strengthening it) to insure a completely dry investment for pouring.

There is a wide variation in time required to complete the burning cycle. Smaller molds (12 by 18 inches) may be burned out in an eight- to ten-hour cycle, while a larger mold (4 by 5 feet) might require as long as three days. A kiln capable of sustaining a temperature in excess of 1100 degrees Fahrenheit for extended periods of time is required. Gas-fired ceramic kilns are quite satisfactory for this purpose. Some burn-out kilns are designed with openings in the bottom to allow melted wax to drain off into a container. Larger foundries use kilns constructed to receive a cart, upon which investments may be loaded. Such a system greatly facilitates the handling of heavy investments.

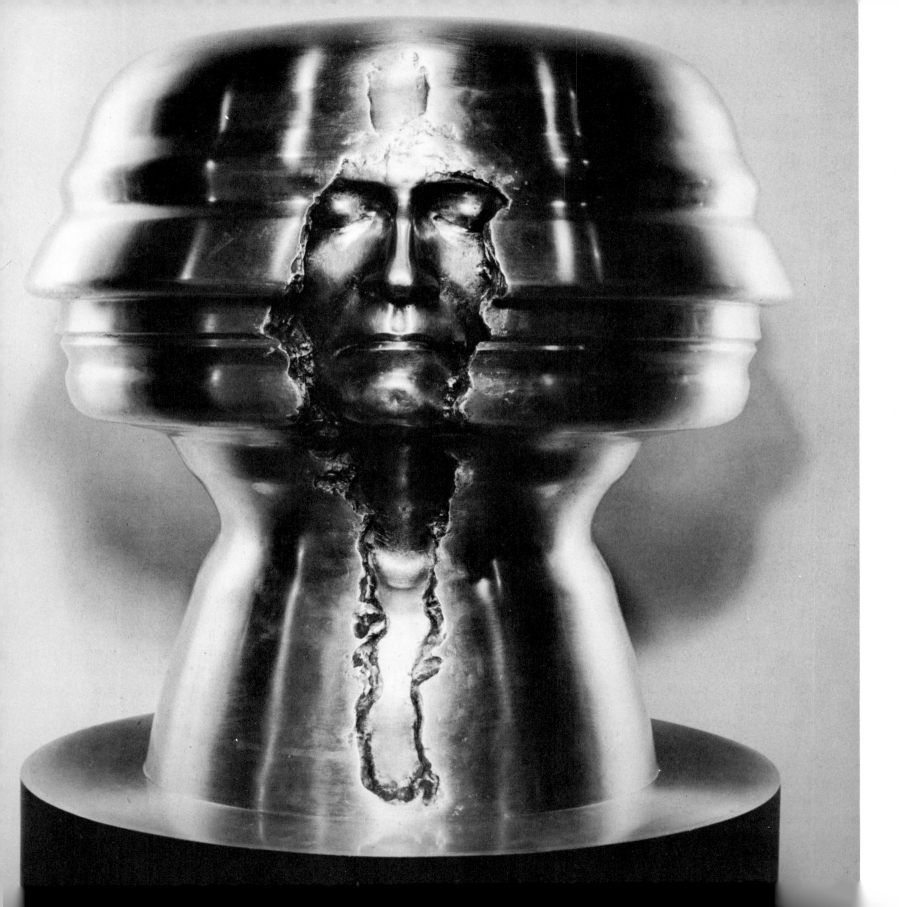

The following are recommended steps in the burn-out procedure:

AIR-DRY — Limited air-dry time is required to set the investment and allow surface moisture to evaporate. Six to eight hours drying time is sufficient for most molds; in most instances it is not desirable to overdry molds prior to burn-out. If a mold must stand overnight or longer, it may be wrapped in plastic or sprayed with water to maintain a desired level of moisture for firing. The chief advantage of firing a damp mold is that it reduces the degree to which wax can penetrate the investment. Moisture in the investment material forms a barrier against such penetration as the wax melts.

MELT-OUT — The bulk of the invested wax may be melted out of the mold at relatively low temperatures, since most modeling waxes melt at 160 degrees or less. Wax expands as it is heated and must be allowed to run off before it cracks the mold. Sprues made from wax of a lower melting point than that of the modeling wax will run off first and allow heat to penetrate to the pattern before it expands. Wax may also be removed by steam. A simple steam oven may be constructed from a 55-gallon drum and water added to a depth of approximately 3 inches (water should not touch the mold). The drum is then heated to create sufficient steam to melt out most of the wax — a large but somewhat limited version of a pressure cooker. Steam-out prevents excessive wax penetration of the investment. A more common method is to place the damp mold on blocks in a kiln with a reducing atmosphere until the wax is melted out into sump pans on the floor. The pans of melted wax may be removed before kindling temperature is reached.

Investments without drain openings must be placed upside down in the kiln and blocked up with the pouring funnel clear to facilitate run-off of melted wax. A drain in the bottom of the mold will allow the investment to be fired upright with the pouring funnel at the top inside the kiln, permitting a visual check at the end of the burn-out cycle. A drain also allows a passage through the mold for more even penetration of heat and a draft through the cavity, which is essential in burning out materials other than wax. A drain channel 3/8-inch in diameter is usually sufficient and may be plugged with an iron rod prior to pouring.

Above
Charles R. Henry, *Regimen*, 1966. Bronze. Courtesy of the artist. Photo by The Cleveland Museum of Art, Cleveland, Ohio.
Opposite
Harold Tovish, *Vortex,* 1966. Bronze, 66" x 18". Collection of Whitney Museum of American Art, New York, Gift of an anonymous donor and purchase. Photo by Geoffrey Clements.
Below
Gio Pomodoro, *Grande Folla*, 1963. Bronze, 31" x 57". Courtesy of Marlborough-Gerson Gallery, New York. Photo by D. E. Nelson.

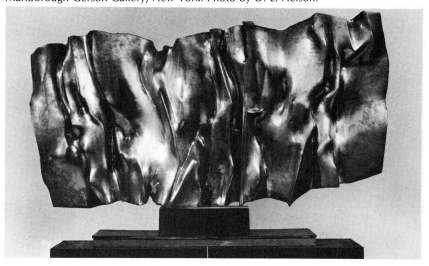

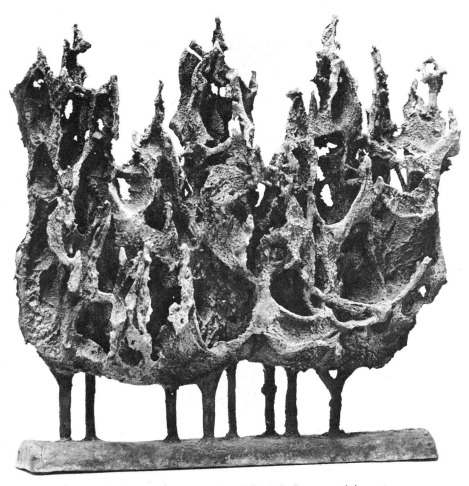

Sylvia Hyman, *Trees of Bronze*, 1965. 12" x 18". Courtesy of the artist.

THE FIRE — Wax residue remaining in the mold cavity is completely eliminated in the fire, moisture is driven off and the investment calcined. Melt-out and burn-out are often accomplished in the same fire. Microcrystalline waxes burn clean and are not detrimental to most gas-fired ceramic kilns designed for reduction fire. When the bulk of invested wax has stopped dripping from openings in the mold, the kiln atmosphere is changed to an oxidizing condition. A temperature rise at a rate of 100 to 150 degrees per hour is established, until a maximum of between 1000 and 1300 degrees Fahrenheit is reached. The rate of fire, maximum temperature, and length of firing time depends upon the size of the mold and the bulk of the wax pattern. Firing temperature must be held until complete burn-off of wax or other materials of the mold is achieved.

Plaster base investments hold up quite well at sustained temperatures up to 1500 degrees Fahrenheit. It is not advisable to exceed this temperature, since most molding plasters begin to break down at 1650 to 1700 degrees. When discoloration disappears from around the pouring funnel and all openings in the mold cease to give off flame or smoke, burn-out is complete. The kiln is then turned off to cool slowly.

Thermal shock is the most common cause of investment breakdown. If a damp investment is placed in a hot kiln, water vapor may be created and crack the mold. Removing a mold that is still at a high temperature to the open air may cause fractures, which will show up as flashing on the sculpture.

Ralph Brown, *Marquette for Confluence*, 1966. Cast aluminum.

Foundry Procedure

Consistent quality in casting requires an efficient and uniform foundry procedure. Weeks or months of work on a piece of sculpture can be destroyed in a few moments by inadequate planning or poor preparation. Each sculptor-founder must develop a system based on the foundry equipment and layout and his own needs. Once he has established a foundry operation that produces a predictable result he should maintain it as the standardized base from which experimentation and invention develop. The sculptor's foundry is not merely a place where a model of sculpture is mechanically reproduced — a commercial foundry can do that. It is an extention of the artist's studio, where the final processes in the production of sculpture occur.

MELT — In most small foundries the metal will be melted in a crucible furnace fired by gas or oil. Controls for the flow of both fuel and air are necessary to adequately govern the furnace atmosphere. The furnace must be top-loading, with access for charging the crucible while it is being fired. Metal of a known alloy or composition should be used; a studio foundry will often select one alloy and use that exclusively to reduce the possibility of mixing scrap and contaminating the melt.

Preheating bronze with a torch to burn off excessive moisture and oil. Photos by University of South Florida, Division of Educational Resources, Tampa, Florida.

Checking temperature of metal with a hand-held pyrometer.

Mixing alloys and using scrap of unknown composition can create many problems and result in serious casting error. The most positive results occur when the melt contains a majority of new metal in ingot form supplemented by scrap of the same composition from previous castings.

The metal to be melted must be clean, dry, and free of grease or oil. Preheating of both crucible and metal will insure a dry charge and burn off oil and other impurities on the surface of the metal. Water may create an explosive condition in the crucible. An ingot must be completely dry before it is added to the melt. Melting should be accomplished as quickly as possible in a neutral furnace atmosphere to avoid exposure of the molten metal to hot gasses and reduce the possibility of picking up gas from the furnace. Bronze and aluminum oxidize at high temperatures and form slag, then their flow characteristics change. The fuel-to-air ratio determines a re-

Placing investments which have been burned out in pouring pit.

ducing or oxidizing condition in the furnace. Excess fuel produces a reducing atmosphere, forming soot and impurities which may contaminate the melt. Excess air produces an oxidizing atmosphere, which increases the formation of oxides on the surface of the metal. The air-fuel mixture may be adjusted to produce tongues of flame above the furnace opening which have a slightly green tinge. A distinct green flame, however, indicates an oxidizing condition, and air should be reduced until the green color is barely evident.

A minimum holding time for molten metal is desirable. If bronze is exposed to a temperature above 2300 degrees Fahrenheit for any extended length of time, the volume of castable metal will reduce considerably. Not only will gases form but the alloying metals, zinc and tin, may burn out; the bronze will then become sluggish and a poor pour will result. Benvenuto Cellini wrote of this problem: When he was casting his *Perseus,* the fire in the melting furnace slowed and the metal curdled (a condition described as "being caked"). By rebuilding the fire to intense heat, he was able to melt the bronze again but it did not flow as rapidly as usual, "the reason being probably that the fierce heat of the fire we kindled had consumed its base alloy." (*The Life of Benvenuto Cellini,* Trans. John Addington Symons. New York: Liverwright Publishing Corp., 1931.)

Rapid melting, minimum holding time, and a neutral or slightly oxidizing atmosphere will produce the most desirable condition of molten metal for pouring.

Flux for Bronze. Traditional foundrymen and sculptor-founders vary widely in their opinions regarding flux for bronze — whether it is needed, what its purpose is, and what kind should be used. The essential purpose of fluxing is to protect the molten metal from impurities and to improve its pouring characteristics. Glass (usually from a broken bottle) has been a popular fluxing agent, and at times in the past some forms of sand have been used. Some foundries use crucible covers to protect against the absorption of gas. Contemporary sculptor-founders in small art foundries recommend that glass, flux, and crucible covers be eliminated, since most commercially available bronze is free of contamination and slag, if it does develop, will float and may be skimmed off.

Any material other than metal added to the melt may end

Lifting crucible containing the molten metal from the melt furnace. Photos by University of South Florida, Division of Educational Resources, Tampa, Florida.

up in the casting as an impurity. Phos-copper (commercially available as 15 percent phosphorus copper) in the form of shot is, in most instances, the only additive needed and should be introduced to the melt just before pouring. It improves the pouring characteristics of molten bronze by reducing the formation of tin oxide and providing a protective coating on the surface. (Approximately 4-6 ounces of phos-copper per 100 pounds bronze are the proportions.)

POUR — Pouring is the most critical operation in the casting process. It must provide a continuous uninterrupted stream of molten metal at the pouring funnel, sufficient in quantity and rate of flow to maintain a reservoir. The stream of metal should be directed to one of the flat sides of the pyramidal shaped pouring funnel to prevent swirling and the entrapment of air.

It is difficult to establish a general temperature guide for pouring bronze. In most instances, it is recommended that the pour be made at the lowest feasible temperature for the cavity

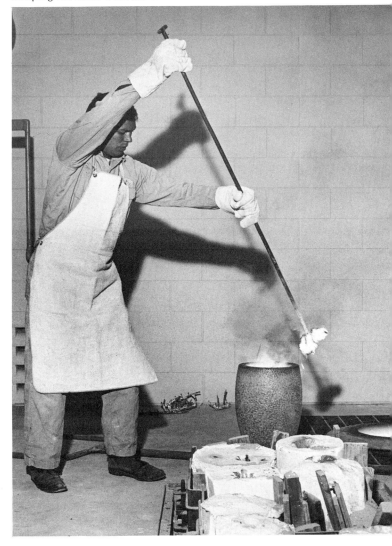

Scraping the dross from the surface of molten metal.

to be filled, but no lower than 100 degrees above the melting point of the metal. For pouring a large melt, thin sections, or cold mold, temperatures from 200 to 300 degrees higher may be required. Overheated metals filling large cavities may cause shrinkage problems. For this reason it is necessary to provide sufficient metal adjacent to the heavy section through large runners and adequate risers to offset excessive shrinkage. After some experience, the sculptor-founder develops a sense of pouring readiness from the motion of the molten metal and the shiny surface he sees under slag or dross. A hand-held pyrometer, which may be inserted directly into the molten metal while it is in the furnace, is a valuable instrument for determining accurate pouring temperatures. After the pour, excess metal may be emptied into an investment well or ingot mold for later use as scrap. The crucible is then replaced in the warm furnace to cool slowly.

SOME COMMON FAULTS — Misrun — The mold cavity is only partially filled, due to freezing of the molten metal in a small runner or insufficient total quantity of metal.

Cold shut — Lines of separation or cracks occur in the casting. They result from interrupted pouring, pouring temperature too low for the pattern thickness, or sluggish metal caused by impurities which reduce fluidity.

Excessive shrinkage — Shrinkage is usually due to insufficient feed to heavy sections of the casting. It is often a problem with very thick and very thin sections in the same piece and can be corrected with proper spruing.

Excessive slag — Poor furnace atmosphere (highly oxidizing condition) or extended holding time at high temperature will produce excessive slag.

Weak-coarse structure — Small fissures or a coarse structure in the casting may result from contamination of the bronze melt by aluminum. Bronze scrap should be kept clean of aluminum. Crucibles are not interchangeable. Bronze and aluminum crucibles should be kept separate.

Gas holes — Hydrogen dissolved during melting from wet metal or a damp furnace surface is forced out as a gas during cooling when it is trapped and a bubble forms just below the surface of the casting. This problem is quickly identified when round holes surrounded by a bright metal surface appear.

Pouring.

CRUCIBLES — Crucibles are the containers in which metals are melted for most foundry procedures. Designed to withstand high temperatures, they are somewhat fragile and require careful treatment to insure long life. When a crucible is charged, metal should not be wedged, forced, or dropped into it. If required, additional amounts of metal may be added to the melt while it is in the furnace. A crucible which has been dropped or struck should be carefully examined for cracks or other signs of weakness before it is used. Molten metal in a split or cracked crucible creates an extremely dangerous foundry condition.

A new crucible may be annealed by slowly bringing it to a temperature of approximately 500 degrees Fahrenheit in its furnace and allowing it to cool gradually without removing it. Both the crucible and its contents must be dry before they are placed in the melt furnace; preheating is advisable to drive off excess moisture.

"Teapot" or spout crucibles allow the molten metal to be poured from the bottom, an advantage in pouring bronze because slag or dross floats. Crucibles with bottom openings and plugs are also available for special applications.

1. Burned out investment placed in wooden frame and reinforced by loosely tamped sand. 2. Preheating scrap bronze prior to adding it to melt. 3. Phos-copper added as a deoxidizer near end of melt cycle. 4. Hand-held pyrometer used to determine correct pouring temperature. 5. Crucible containing molten bronze removed from melt furnace and placed in pouring shank.

DIVESTING — When the pour is complete, the investment should be allowed to cool slowly before the casting is taken out of the mold. Large sections of investment may be broken away with a hammer and large cold chisel, smaller areas and cores will require special tools. A variety of tools for the removal of investment may be fabricated from steel rod. Points, picks — both straight and curved, hoe-shaped hand tools and scrapers are among those most useful in the somewhat tedious job of scraping away the fire-hardened plaster. Large bolt cutters may be used to remove the sprue system to free bound investment. Wire brushes will remove investment from the surface of the casting so that it will not be driven into the pores of the metal surface during chasing. Sandblasting equipment is also used to remove remnants of investment and to clean the fire scale from the surface of the casting.

The divesting process produces quantities of used plaster-based investment called luto. Luto is an excellent refractory material and may be ground into a grog for use in future investments. A separate studio area is often required to accommodate the quantity of dust produced; an active foundry will require special arrangements for removal of mold waste.

CHASING — Chasing is the finishing or tooling of the cast surface to impart a detailed modeling or texture. The sprue system must be removed, holes left by core pins filled, and casting imperfections repaired. Gates should be sawed off slightly above the finish surface then filed, ground, or tooled to achieve the desired effect. A gate which was flattened into a rectangular shape at the point where it attached to the wax model will facilitate removal because when cast in bronze it will bend before distorting or damaging the cast. A sprue system design which places the gates and vents on high or convex surfaces where they are accessible for finishing, will greatly reduce problems at this time. Core-pin holes or bubbles may be repaired by drilling and tapping the hole and screwing in a plug made from a short length of sprue which has been threaded. An inexpensive tap and die set will perform the task quite nicely. An oxy-acetylene torch or argon arc are invaluable instruments for repairing or rebuilding surfaces. This is discussed in the chapter on welding and brazing.

6

7

8

6. Skimming dross from surface of molten bronze. 7. Pouring an even, uninterrupted flow of molten metal delivered to pouring funnel of investment. 8. Divesting: Bolt cutters are used to cut away the sprue system once the majority of investment material has been removed.

105

Tony Padovano, *Interlocking Forms*, 1967. Cast bronze, 7¼" x 8½" x 5¼". Courtesy of Bertha Schaefer Gallery, New York. Photo by William Brevoort.

Casting—Ceramic-Shell, Self-Cure Sand

CERAMIC-SHELL CASTING

Ceramic-shell casting, a modern industrial equivalent to the *cire-perdue* process, has been developed to meet the exacting requirements of precision investment casting. There are many advantages to using the ceramic shell for casting sculpture of a limited size. The mold is quite thin and light for easy handling and it has the strength of fired clay. It is possible to achieve finer detail and surface finishes than with more conventional investments. A high resistance to thermal shock permits rapid temperature changes and higher firing temperatures and, as a consequence, the elimination of a wider variety of pattern materials. A major advantage to using the ceramic shell is the greatly reduced time of the burn-out cycle: small molds may be burned out in as little as one-half hour, and the largest size recommended for this process, one dimension approximately 24 inches, should not require a burn-out cycle of more than four hours.

The model or pattern of the sculpture to be cast may be developed using the methods of the lost wax process. Wax is the most popular material for construction of the pattern, due to the higher temperatures possible in burn-out. A wider variety of materials would include wood, paper, plastics, or almost anything which will burn out leaving little or no residue in the mold cavity. When the model to be burned out is constructed of materials which leave ash or residue, openings for

Sculpture by Alfred Charley using the ceramic shell process. Plastic toys used as models were burned out at relatively high temperatures and cast in bronze.

a draft in the mold should be arranged. At the end of the burn-out cycle a blast of compressed air through the mold cavity will effectively clear such residue and the draft hole may then be plugged.

The sculptor's primary concern is for the visual and tactile qualities of the casting; therefore highly technical considerations of shrinkage tolerance and casting density of the industrial founder need not apply. The sculptor may abbreviate the process recommended for industry, take short cuts, develop his own techniques and still produce quality castings with considerable savings in time and labor.

Sprue System

Gating and spruing of a model for the ceramic-shell mold may be highly simplified, often consisting of simply a pouring funnel attached directly to the model. The pour may be made directly through the mold by top-pouring, thereby avoiding the outside sprue system required by bottom-pouring methods. The ceramic shell is sufficiently strong to withstand the weight of heavy molten metals without cracking or washing away. It is also porous enough so that trapped air and gas may escape, making vents unnecessary; the closed mold also provides a slight back pressure to insure that metal reaches and fills all cavities of the mold.

Metal from the pouring funnel is usually sufficient to feed casting shrinkage as the casting freezes. More complex shapes may require the installation of sprues to feed shrinkage of large cavities which cannot be fed directly by the pouring funnel. When the complexity of the model is such that wax does not readily run out of some sections during melt-out, drains from such trapped areas to the pouring funnel will be required; they may be plugged after burn-out.

Investment

All surfaces of the model must be clean and free of grease or oil in order that the investment, in the form of a slurry, may adhere to it. A cleaning and wetting agent such as liquid detergent or a specially prepared pattern cleaner is used for this purpose. A wash of acetone followed by a wash of 5 percent alcohol-shellac may also be used. It is important that the slurry of the first coat adhere to the entire model. If there are some "holidays," or bare spots, wash off the slurry with water and reclean the model.

The shell is built up with a series of continuous ceramic layers starting with a wetting slurry coat followed by a dry refractory. The slurry, which has been mixed in a plastic or stainless steel container (not galvanized because of a possible reaction with the binders in the slurry), is applied by dipping or pouring it, allowing it to drain completely and then sprinkling the shell with a refractory grog or silica grain. To prevent its being washed off the stuccoed layer is allowed to dry thoroughly before the next layer is applied. The slurry, a water suspension of fine refractory and binder, must be constantly stirred to prevent settling. A consistency of heavy cream is desirable for most applications. Three coatings will be required to produce a minimum mold thickness of $1/4$ inch. Thicker molds, up to $1/2$ inch, will reduce the danger of cracking from rough handling or wax expansion. The model configuration should determine mold thickness, unsupported extensions may be reinforced with fiberglass cloth or stainless steel wire between the outer layers of the ceramic mold.

Burn-out

The wax model must be quickly melted out of the mold at a high temperature to prevent any expansion of wax from cracking the ceramic shell. If heated quickly, a liquid film will form on all wax shell surfaces before the mass of wax can expand. A number of methods are available to supply the concentrated heat necessary for melt-out. Infrared radiation lamps played directly on the mold surface will penetrate the shell and be absorbed by a thin layer of wax, creating a fluid surface on the model. Infrared penetration of the wax is gradual, allowing the surface to melt and run off without melting the bulk of the model and thus reducing the possibility of expansion. A heated iron rod inserted through the pouring funnel and down into the solid wax of the main sprue and model will create an interior channel to take up some of the expanding wax. A gas torch, readily available in most sculpture studios, may also be used to de-wax ceramic shell molds. The ceramic shell is placed upside down on a metal grate and the concentrated heat of the torch directed at the pouring channel. A small area of wax will melt and run off, making room for the expanding wax above. The torch is then directed to an adjacent area on the exterior of the shell mold and the process continued until the point farthest from the pouring funnel is free of the wax mass. The ceramic shell will withstand severe thermal shock and when wax expansion is not an important consideration it may be placed directly into a kiln preheated to 1000 degrees Fahrenheit for rapid melting.

After the wax has drained, the shell is ready for burn-out to remove completely all wax residue. The mold is placed in a burn-out oven or kiln at 1300 to 1800 degrees Fahrenheit for a period ranging from thirty minutes to two hours, depending upon the size and complexity of the pattern. Burn-out is complete when there is no smoke from mold openings and the pouring funnel is free of soot.

SELF-CURE OR SELF-SETTING SAND CASTING

The casting industry has long sought a binder for sand as a mold material in the sand-casting process. An ideal binder would reduce the size and weight of investments, eliminate the time and equipment requirements of the traditional bake-cure system, and produce sizable cores for larger castings. Considerable research has now produced a new resin-base, no-bake binder for sand with properties that improve core-making and molding and are highly adaptable to the needs of the studio foundry.

This two-component self-curing binder was originally developed for steel casting operations to overcome problems in bake-curing large cores, and it has many advantages for the sculptor. The air-setting, bonded mold retains the characteristic porosity of sand. Gases are easily eliminated during the pour and spruing systems are therefore reduced to a minimum. The strength of the resin binder permits the use of relatively light piece-molds (between 2 and 3 inches thick) which may be separated for the removal of the pattern, thus eliminating the necessity for melt-out of the pattern as well as bake-curing of the mold. The piece-mold may be reassembled and wired or clamped together for the pour. Many variations are possible with this process, from carving directly in pre-cast blocks of sand to using ready-made objects as patterns for components of sculpture.

The self-curing sand process utilizes a silica sand which is mixed or mulled with a resin binder and activated by a resin catalyst with a cure time at room temperature (60 to 80 degrees Fahrenheit) in approximately twenty-four hours. The exceptional strength of the mold material permits direct pouring of the molten aluminum or bronze into an assembled piece-mold without the necessity of backing up the mold with tamped sand in a pit or frame. In those instances where a piece-mold is not desirable, the resin-bonded sand will withstand sustained temperature of more than 450 degrees for melt-out of wax patterns.

1

2

1. White silica sand measured by weight. 2. Self-cure resin one and one-half percent weight of sand. 3. Ingredients are mulled in converted cement mixer and catalyst added (self-cure additive number two). 4. Mix removed from mulling machine.

3

4

Sprue System

The high porosity retained by the sand in the self-cure system eliminates the complicated sprue, vent, and gating required for most plaster binder investments. A single heavy sprue with pouring funnel for a top pour and single vent are all that are required except for the most complicated pattern configurations. The pouring funnel and a similar size well on the vent will provide a sufficient quantity of metal to feed shrinkage as the metal cools. Where a piece-mold is used, the top plate of the mold may be drilled and a pre-cast pouring funnel attached with mold cement to receive the molten metal.

Mulling

A thorough mixing or mulling of all components of the sand investment material is necessary to insure an even consistency and smooth mold surface. For this, the sculptor needs a mulling machine capable of mixing a minimum of 100 pounds of sand (a cement mixer with mixing blades removed and square or rectangular weights placed in the mixing drum serves as an adequate mulling machine in a small studio foundry). The mulling machine is charged with dry silica sand of sufficient quantity for the first sections of the piece-mold. If dry additives are used (clay, or red iron oxide for hot strength in bronze pouring, approximately 1 percent by weight) dry mull for a few minutes before adding resin. Resin binder is added in proportion to the total amount of sand — 2 percent binder to sand, by weight. Thorough mixing of the sand and binder is necessary to coat each grain of sand and eliminate "wet spots," or unmixed binder. Two to four minutes mulling time, depending upon quantity of mixture, is normally sufficient. The catalyst is then added to the mixture, 20 percent by weight of the *resin binder,* and the mixture mulled two to four minutes. Over-mulling should be avoided at this point and the sand mixture used immediately. The mix begins to set up approximately ten minutes after the catalyst has been added; at room temperature it has a working time not longer than an hour, depending on binder formulation.

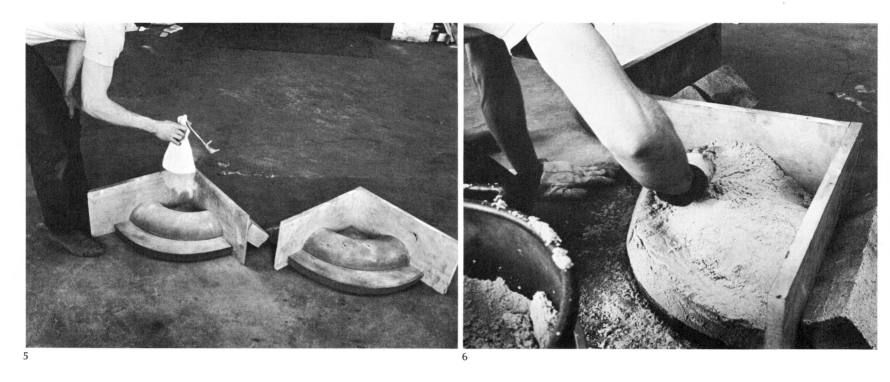

5

6

5. Parting compound (powdered talc) is sprinkled on the pattern. 6. Sand is hand-packed into pattern box. 7. After twenty-four hours cure time, molds are removed from pattern box. 8. Interior mold surfaces are lined with plasteline or felt to desired thickness of final casting.

7

8

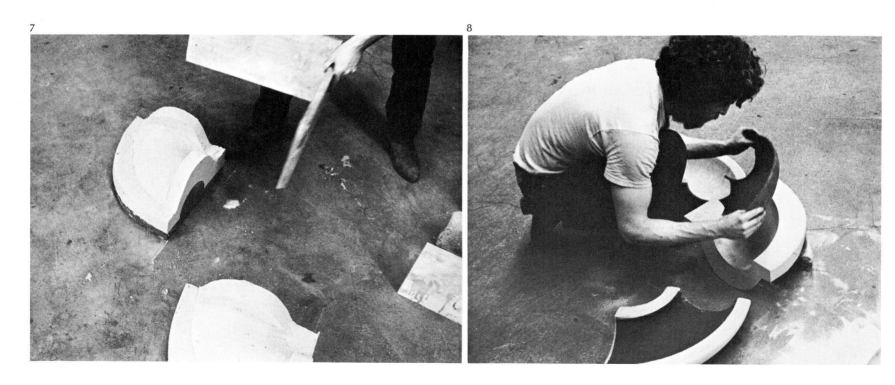

9

10

9. Sections of mold are reassembled and with liner in place the core is packed. 10. Registration marks are used on all mold sections for ease in reassembly. 11. Mold sections are separated and lining material removed. 12. Three sections of mold showing the interlocking core and base-plate.

11

12

13. Mold wash is used on core to provide hot strength.

Completing the Mold

Sections of a piece-mold may be hand packed over a pattern in a pattern box or directly on the model. Dividers between the sections of the mold may be made from old photographic negatives cut to the contour of the pattern and held in place by plastic clay. Twenty-four hours cure time is required for the first sections to set-up, after which the mold dividers are removed. Parting compound (powdered talc) is sprinkled on all surfaces which will come in contact with the fresh sand of the next section. When the exterior sections of the mold are set and marked for registration they are separated and the pattern removed. Interior surfaces of the mold are lined with plasteline or felt to the desired thickness of the final casting and the core is packed. Most piece-molds for casting require an interlocking core which is used for a base in assembling the mold. Narrow core sections may be reinforced with steel rod or wire mesh. The formula for cores should include a 2 or 3 percent addition of wood flour to permit easy removal from the casting. When the core has set, the mold is taken apart and the pattern-forming material is removed.

Once the mold is complete and ready to be assembled for the pour, a mold cement is used to bond sections of the mold;

they may also be clamped or wired together. Pouring-gate and vent holes may be drilled and pre-cast pouring funnels attached — the reservoir on both gate and vent should be large enough to feed shrinkage as the metal cools.

A number of applications are possible with this system. It is possible to invest a wax model by hand packing it with self-setting sand to a thickness of 2 or 3 inches and then melting out the wax in a manner similar to that used for plaster base investments. Since the binder breaks down at a sustained tem-

14. Mold wash ignited.

114

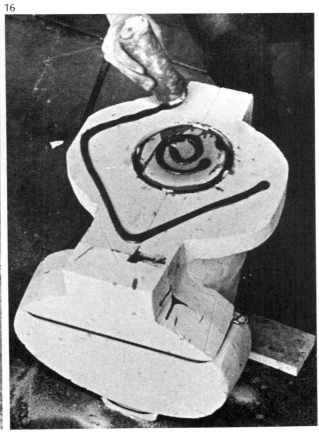

16

15. Mold sections reassembled and held in place by wire. 16. Mold cement is used to adhere the cover-plate. 17. Pouring funnels are molded separately and attached to cover-plate with mold cement. One-inch-diameter holes are drilled through cover-plate to provide a single heavy sprue and vent. 18. Assembled molds with cover-plate and pouring funnels are placed in position ready for pour. Paper discs cover pouring funnel to prevent dust and other contamination from entering mold.

17

19

19. Pour. 20. Exterior sections of mold are removed quite easily. The core contains a small percentage of wood flour which facilitates its removal. 21. Completed casting with sprues attached. 22. *Opposite* Cast elbow sections were welded together by the T I G process to provide the reverse curves in the finished sculpture by Peter Volkos. It resulted from a three-day workshop at the University of Kentucky.

20

21

perature of approximately 450 degrees, a slight wax residue will remain in the mold. This residue is driven off through the porous sand mold by the molten metal during pour.

The sand investment may be carved and shaped with a variety of tools to form the basic shape for a piece of sculpture. The shape is used for the core and the final form modeled in oil-base clay or wax over it. Once the final form is achieved, the outer sections of the mold are built up (in sections for a piece-mold or in one piece if the wax is to be melted out), the pattern material removed, and the mold is ready for casting. This variation of the process provides a direct and quick method quite suitable for students in a classroom situation.

SELF-CURE BINDER

SELF-CURE FORMULATION (SERIES 1531)	APPLICATIONS	WORKING TIME (min.)	STRIP TIME (min.)	FULL-CURE TIME (hrs.)	SAND TEMP. (°F.)	AIR TEMP. (°F.)
W - 3	Three basic formulations	35 - 40	60 - 70	24	76	76
W - 6	for general foundry use.	25 - 30	40 - 50	24	76	76
W - 10		10	25 - 30	24	76	76

TYPICAL SAND MIX

SAND	WEIGHT (lbs.)	SELF-CURE RESIN (lbs.)	MULLING TIME (min.)	SELF-CURE ADDITIVE NO. 2 (lbs.)	MULLING TIME (min.)
Silica-lake, bank, dune (AFS 45-60)	1000	15 (1-1½ % wt. of sand)	1-2	3 (20 % wt. of resin)	2-3

NOTE: Mulling time for Simpson, Clearfield, and paddle-type mullers, based on 70°F. sand, air temperatures.
Courtesy of International Minerals and Chemical Corporation, Skokie, Illinois

22

The Foundry Installation

8

Numerous studio foundries have been developed as a result of the manner in which many contemporary sculptors work — that is, in direct control of each stage or process which affects their sculpture. The exorbitant costs of casting sculpture in a commercial foundry and the availability of casting materials and equipment developed by industry are additional factors which have caused many sculptors and students to become their own foundrymen. Establishing a foundry capable of producing sophisticated results is not a difficult task, but the foundry operation does involve considerable manual labor in hot dusty conditions. And handling quantities of molten metal and moving heavy bulky investments can be dangerous if a few basic considerations of safety are not met.

Ventilation is important. Molten bronze or aluminum give off quantities of fumes, some toxic, and adequate ventilation or an outside installation of the foundry is a prime consideration. Dry conditions are needed, for moisture — damp sand or a wet floor — are extremely dangerous. Water in contact with molten bronze creates an explosive situation; a wet charge or wet additive to a melt are also hazardous. A dry, tamped earth or sand floor or a metal grating over sand will retard the flow of molten metal spilled from a dropped or cracked crucible. Safety clothing should be worn — hard cotton twill coveralls, asbestos leggings, founders sleeves and apron, leather scull cap, gloves, plastic face mask, and heavy shoes provide the necessary protection for individuals involved in the pouring operation.

Other factors for consideration when establishing a foundry are: proximity of burn-out ovens and pouring areas; availability of gas (natural or bottled); the disposal of large quantities of used investment; gantry on wheels with chain hoist or other system for moving heavy investments and to support heavy melts during the pour.

Placing crucible containing molten bronze in pouring shank. Photo by Don Irving.

An Inexpensive Foundry

An inexpensive foundry for the initial experiments in casting by the sculptor in his own studio or in an educational situation where economy is a prime factor has many advantages. It is a valuable means of confronting basic casting problems using traditional foundry techniques. Without automatic equipment and sensitive temperature measurement, the founder must rely on sound and appearance of flame for the adjustment of the gas-air ratio. He must learn to recognize the appearance of molten metal and develop a sense of readiness for pouring. What an inexpensive foundry lacks in accuracy and efficiency it more than makes up for as a place to gain an understanding of the processes and to experiment with them. It is also a sound way of determining special needs and the capacity of a foundry before installing expensive equipment.

If the foundry is to be set up indoors, a large-capacity exhaust system with adequate hoods over melt furnace and pouring pit are required. Outside installations eliminate the considerable problems of ventilation. The foundry floor (that area where molten metal will be handled) should be raised steel grating or sand-covered to a depth of 4 inches to con-

Inexpensive foundry.

tain the flow of spilled molten metal. A sand pit in which to pack investments is desirable for two reasons. First, molten metal escaping through a crack in the investment cannot spread on the foundry floor; and second, the pouring funnel in the investment is close to the floor level so that the hot crucible with molten metal will not need to be raised more than a few inches for pouring. In those installations where a pit is not feasible, casting rings or wooden frames may be used. The investment is placed in the frames, which are built up in sections, and sand is tamped loosely around it as a reinforcement.

A simple foundry capable of producing sophisticated results may be constructed from materials readily available to most sculptors. The basic piece of equipment is the melt furnace which will accommodate a crucible in which the metal is melted. The furnace illustrated was made from a 55-gallon steel drum with 8 inches cut from one end and it was lined with refractory cement to a thickness of approximately 3½ inches. A platform 10 inches in diameter was built up to a height of 2 inches from the floor of the furnace to form a pedestal, upon which the crucible rests. The lid of the furnace was made from the section cut from the drum. Reinforcing rods were welded across the shallow cylinder to support and contain the refractory cement lining. A tight fit between the lid and the top lip of the furnace may be assured by casting the lid in place and using wax paper as a parting agent.

When the lid is cast, register marks may be welded to the outside of both lid and furnace for correct alignment when the lid is replaced. Two loops or rings on the top edge of the lid receive the steel pipe used to lift it. An opening for an exhaust port 5 inches in diameter was left in the center of the lid. Fire brick placed over this opening allows for adjustment to the most effective operating size. Burners for the melt furnace were constructed of standard ½-inch pipe and fittings for gas feed with both gas cock and adjustment valve. For the air source, a salvage vacuum cleaner of the industrial type was connected, using auto-radiator hose and 1½ inch pipe and gas cock. (Common household vacuum cleaners have also proved satisfactory; a furnace of this size would require more than one, connected in parallel.) Gas and air were mixed in a tee, attached to the furnace plate by means of three centering bolts threaded through nuts welded to the plate. The mix-

Pouring shank and lifting tongs.

ing tee was centered in the furnace port with a ½-inch opening between tee and interior diameter of port. The burner is set at a slight angle where it enters the furnace to create an even, circular flow of flame and heat around the interior.

Crucible tongs and pouring shank were constructed from 1½-inch scrap pipe, ½-inch steel rod and ¼-inch flat steel stock. The ring on the pouring shank and jaws of the tongs must be carefully fitted to the contour of the crucible.

Detail of burners.

Ruth Vollmer, *Monomer-Dimer-Dimer-Primer*, no date. Cast bronze, 13″ diameter spheres. Courtesy of Betty Parsons Gallery, New York.

College Foundry

Many college art departments, recognizing an inter-dependence between sculpture and foundry technique, demand that the student in sculpture work directly with his materials as his own foundryman. Such programs involve the installation of a foundry of considerable capacity and versatility. The foundry must be capable of melting bronze and other metals in sufficient quantity for the largest work anticipated. It must be able to handle the metal safely and to cast it, using as many as possible of the standard molding techniques. A leading foundry supply company has prepared the following proposal for a sculpture casting installation adequate to the needs of a university sculpture program.

Two hundred and fifty pounds of bronze has been chosen as a limiting capacity; lost wax, sand, and ceramic shell processes are suggested as standard techniques. Larger pieces may be assembled from individual 250-pound casts, and other techniques may be developed using variations and combinations of the standard techniques. The foundry is set up with commercially available equipment and is planned to use readily available supplies from foundry supply houses. Two melting furnaces are suggested for the rapid and economical melting of various quantities, the smallest being 30 pounds of bronze and the largest 250 pounds of bronze. A large floor-type oven is suggested for de-waxing molds in the lost wax process. A high temperature burn-out kiln is proposed for the firing of lost wax molds.

Lifting and handling equipment to permit safe and easy handling of the heavy molds and crucibles will be required as will venting and dust control equipment and a source of compressed air.

Lyman Kipp, *21 February 1966.* Bronze, 12" x 24" x 3". Courtesy of Betty Parsons Gallery, New York.

Sculpture Casting Installation

1. *Melting and Pouring Aluminum, Bronze, Gray Iron*
   Furnaces — 30-200 lbs. bronze: McEnglevan B-70 with blower; 250 lbs. bronze: Campbell-Hausfeld tilting furnace, 800 GT with Hausfeld blower.
   Tongs — vertical lift tong for #10, #20, and #30 crucible.
   Safety equipment — 12 pr. 14″ asbestos lined gloves; 12 pr. sleeves-chrome leather; 12 pr. spats; 12 visors.
2. *Melting Wax*
   Hones 72-18 gas hot plate
   Stay-warm wax dropper
   Safety equipment — 12 pr. 14″ rubber gloves; 12 pr. glasses.
3. *Plaster Molding*
   Lightning mixer NDIA with portable stand.
   Safety equipment — 12 aprons.
4. *Rubber Molding*
   Hones 72-18 gas hot plate.
   Metalsmith's batch can 20 gal.
5. *Sand Molding*
   12 24″ x 24″ x 12″ flasks.
   12 36″ x 36″ x 14″ flasks.
6. *Mold Firing and De-waxing*
   Grieve Handy Oven 54″ x 72″ x 72″ with mold truck temperature to 650° with Partlow indicating limit control.
7. *Burn-out*
   Demountable kiln with 4 VNB-200 gas burners — max size: 48″ x 60″ x 60″; temperature limit 1500°F. with pyrometer.
8. *Shell Molding*
   2 TM #30 turntable mixers.
   2 fluidized beds.
   Drop bottom furnace 20″ dia. x 24″ high with 2 VNB-200 gas burners.

9. *Handling*
   2 1-ton hoists.
   4 mold carts.
   Allowance for chains and iron work.
10. *Finishing*
    Rough cleaning knock-out air hammer.
    Hand grinder.
    Sand blast — Dust booth 72″ x 84″ x 60″; portable sand blast gun.
    Safety Equipment — 2 pulmosan hoods; 6 glasses.
11. *General*
    Air compressor 15 h. p.
    Venting-allow.
    Dust collector-pressure blast.
12. *Supplies*
    Modeling wax — Mobil #2300.
    Casting wax — Saunders Blue.
    Modeling clay — oil-base.
    Modeling clay — ceramic.
    Molding plaster.
    Casting plaster.
    Ceramic shell — Supercast A, B, C, D; Syton Binder.
    Styrofoam — logs 7″ x 22″ x 12″.
    Crucibles (regular graphite) — #10, #20, #30, #60, #80.

courtesy of Alexander Saunders & Co., Inc., New York

Opposite
Ruth Vollmer, *Slipped Hemisphere*, 1966-67. Spun copper.

Michael Hall, *Mastodon* Series,
Installation of an exhibition at Vanderbilt University, 1968.

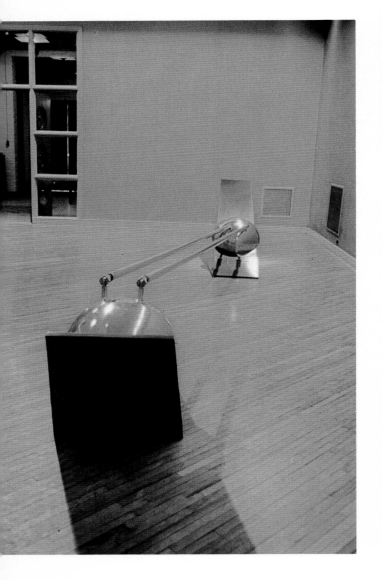

Finishing

9

Finishes for sculpture serve many purposes, from the protection of a sculptural surface from the elements in outside installations to the acceleration of the natural corrosive action of the atmosphere for a desired effect. Most traditional finishing procedures were designed to enhance the nature of the sculptural material and correlate to its setting or purpose. Renaissance bronzes, for example, were buried in the earth for long periods of time to develop a patina suitable for outside installations. Bronze castings were also buried in manure piles to achieve the desired corrosive surface quickly and overcome the fresh or raw appearance of newly cast bronze. Bronze casts for inside installations on the other hand were often polished and lacquered or gold-leafed to achieve a highly refined or slick surface.

Contemporary sculptors have used a wide variety of finishes for sculpture or, in some instances, no finish at all. The polychrome surfaces of much recent sculpture are often as significant to the total piece as the material used or its three-dimensional quality. Much welded steel sculpture is allowed to rust naturally. It is the nature of the material and such deterioration is part of the sculptor's original concept. In some instances, a matrix has been used by sculptors, the principal purpose of which was to receive the plating or sprayed metal deposits of the finish. Many of the industrial finishing techniques used by sculptors require expensive equipment, close technical control, and large operating space. For these and other reasons it is often more convenient to have the plating, anodizing, or sandblasting of a sculpture done at a factory or shop equipped to handle the job. Nevertheless, a working knowledge of such processes and understanding of their capabilities and results is essential to the sculptor who is to use them to full advantage.

The finish applied to the surface of a sculpture is an integral part of the total form concept and is as worthy of consideration as any phase in the construction or development of a piece. A finish may emphasize, highlight, or totally disguise the material used. The nature of the material may be exploited or ignored, depending upon the sculptor's purpose.

Cleaning

An initial stage in the preparation of metal surfaces to receive a finish is cleaning. Fire scale left by welding or casting procedures must be removed. A power-driven flex-shaft tool with a circular wire brush is effective for removing the heavy scale from steel and the remnants of investment from aluminum and bronze. Steel wool and abrasive cleaning compounds may

Flex-shaft tool with wire brush.

be used in hard-to-get-at places. Successive abrasive steps, including sanding and polishing with buffing compounds, may be necessary to remove scratches left by the wire brush and achieve the desired surface.

ACID PICKLING — A "pickle bath" is often used for cleaning both ferrous and non-ferrous metals, particularly after welding, annealing, or other heat treatment. The immersion process requires a glass or non-porous ceramic vessel large enough to accommodate the entire piece. A large sculpture may be cleaned by swabbing with a heavy natural-fiber cloth attached to a length of wooden dowel.

Aluminum. A bright etched finish may be produced on aluminum by first immersing it in an alkaline solution:

    caustic soda or trisodium phosphate — 4 to 8 ounces
    180°F. for four minutes

The alkaline bath will produce a dull surface skin which is then removed by a thirty-second immersion in a bright dip of one part nitric acid and one part water.

Heat stain, which often results from welding aluminum, may be removed by immersion in:

    hydrofluoric acid — 1 part
    nitric acid — 1 part
    water — 98 parts
    room temperature for approximately one minute

Cast aluminum. Cast aluminum, containing various alloying metals such as silicon and iron, develops a surface film of black or brown during the alkaline bath which may be a desirable finish for some sculpture. The alkaline solution dissolves aluminum out of the surface and the alloying metals remain. This film may be removed by immersion in:

    nitric acid — 3 parts
    hydrofluoric acid — 1 part
    room temperature

Copper. The standard pickle for copper and its alloys is:

    sulfuric acid — 1 part
    water — 9 parts
    room temperature or slightly above (125°F.)

Copper and alloys of brass or bronze containing high percentages of copper (more than 85 percent) often develop films of cuprous oxide which are difficult to remove with the standard sulfuric pickle. In such cases the addition of an oxidizing agent is necessary:

    sulfuric acid — 1 pint
    sodium dichromate — 3 ounces
    water — 1 gallon
    room temperature

Heavy fire scale on copper and its alloys is often difficult to remove with the above formulas, particularly if it is to be bright dipped. A fire scale dip consists of:

    sulfuric acid — 2 parts
    nitric acid — 1 part
    water — 2 quarts
    sodium chloride or hydrochloric acid — 1 fluid ounce

If a spotty surface results from the bright dip, it may be necessary to reduce the amount of hydrochloric acid or sodium chloride. Additions of small amounts of activated carbon often improve the bright dip.

If the sculpture is to be lacquered, it should be flushed thoroughly with cold water then dipped in a hot rinse containing 2 ounces of soap per gallon of hot water.

A light matter or dull-dip finish may be produced on copper and copper alloys with the following solution (it should be kept water-free):

    sulfuric acid — 1 gallon
    nitric acid — 1 gallon
    zinc oxide — 1½ pounds

A finer finish may be achieved by increasing the sulfuric acid and a coarser one by increasing the nitric acid.

A dull or surface-etched finish is obtained from:

    hydrochloric acid — 1 part
    40-percent ferric chloride solution — 1 part

If a cloudy film is present after this treatment, a brief immersion in the bright dip above will remove the film, leaving the surface clear and dull.

Iron and Steel. Acid treatment of iron and steel for the removal of fire scale and rust is ordinarily accomplished by the use of sulfuric or hydrochloric acid. Hydrochloric acid has a much more rapid cleaning action than sulfuric acid, however it requires tanks lined with rubber or organic linings which are quite expensive. To minimize pitting of the metal, pickling inhibitors may be required.

For cast iron these solutions may be used:

1. sulfuric acid — 1 part
   hydrofluoric acid — 1 part
   water — 8 parts
2. sulfuric acid — 12 ounces
   nitric acid — 5 ounces
   zinc — 1 ounce
   water — 1 gallon

Effective cleaning solutions for iron and steel are:

1. sulfuric acid — 1 part
   water — 15 parts
2. hydrochloric acid — 1 part
   water — 1 part
3. sulfuric acid — 3 ounces per gallon
   potassium nitrate — 3 ounces per gallon
4. citric acid — 10 ounces per gallon
   ammonia — 2 ounces per gallon

Boil to remove rust; this will have little adverse effect on the metal surface.

Monel metal and nickel cleaning can be accomplished with:

hydrochloric acid — 1 gallon
cupric chloride — ½ pound
water — 2 gallons
temperature 125° to 150°F.

Grinding off imperfections from casting process. Photo by J. Falkoner.

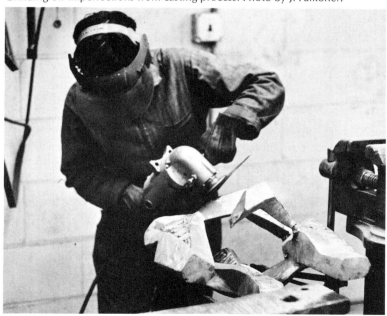

It is possible in some instances to remove excess solder from sculpture of brass, copper, steel, and other metals by dipping in the following solution:

10-percent fluoboric acid (1 part 42-percent HBF; 3 parts water) — 4 parts
30-percent hydrogen peroxide — 6 fluid ounces per gallon
room temperature for five to ten minutes

SANDBLASTING — Sandblasting is a process which involves propelling thousands of abrasive particles at the surface to be cleaned with a high-velocity air stream. It effectively replaces acid bath pickling, brushing, and hand cleaning. In most instances no other cleaning is necessary. The sand removes oily deposits as well as scale and surface contamination, leaving the surface chemically and mechanically clean. Sandblasting also provides a surface "tooth" to improve the bond of paint, plastics, and other surface coatings, and to receive sprayed metal coatings and electrodeposits. It is estimated that the surface area of metal increases as much as ten times as the result of the abrasive's impact action.

There are two types of sandblasting equipment in general use:

Direct Air Pressure. In this equipment the sand abrasive is contained in a pressure vessel and forced to the hand-held blast gun by compressed air at approximately 70 to 90 pounds per square inch. Many direct-pressure types of equipment have additional features including shut-off controls for air and abrasive, adjustable orifices, and multiple chamber arrangements for continuous operation.

Induction Air. In this equipment the abrasive is brought to the blast gun by means of a partial vacuum created by compressed air passing through the gun. The abrasive is sucked into a space between jet and nozzle; there it is mixed with compressed air, which accelerates the movement of each grain. At the nozzle tip the air expands and pressure is transformed into velocity. Induction equipment is generally more satisfactory for cleaning sculpture because of the somewhat lower blast intensity and lower initial and maintenance cost of equipment.

Final finishing. Photo by J. Falkoner.

Electroplating

Electroplating is a process by which thin films of metals such as cadmium, chromium, copper, and nickel are deposited on the surfaces of other metals. Materials other than metal may be electroplated through the use of conductive surface coatings or chemically prepared surfaces. Electroplating is accomplished by means of an electric current passing through a metallic salt solution (usually cyanide compounds). The plating

metal in the form of an anode with wires attached is suspended in the electrolytic bath. Current passes from the immersed anode through the solution, dissolving the metal of the anode and depositing it on the cathode or sculpture to be plated. Electroplating is a precise operation requiring extreme care and carefully regulated safety precautions because of the deadly cyanide compounds that must be handled in preparing most plating formulas. Adequate ventilation of the plating area is a must.

An experimental unit for small copper plating operations may be constructed from materials that are on hand or easily

Eduardo Paolozzi,
Alpha, 1965. Chrome plated steel, 40" x 26½" x 13¾".
Courtesy of Robert Fraser Gallery, London.

Don Irving, *Female Form*, 1964. Steel, brass plated, 22" x 14".

obtainable. A glass tank with the capacity of 2 or more gallons is required; a basket or platform made from copper wire is used to suspend the sculpture in the tank; a sheet of copper with positive wire attached will serve as the anode; wire attached directly to the cleaned sculpture provides the cathode. A 6- or 12-volt battery, rheostat, and voltmeter complete the circuit.

A simple plating arrangement consists of:

Solution
water (pure or distilled) — 1 gallon
sulfuric acid — 5 ounces
copper sulfate — 1½ pounds

Conditions

Current — 5 volts for 5 minutes, reduce to 2 volts; 3 amperes per square foot of cathode; room temperature. Time required for plating varies from fifteen minutes to an hour depending upon thickness of deposit desired. Heavier coatings will require additional time.

Larger plating operations will require somewhat more sophisticated equipment including a transformer if standard electrical current is to be used; tanks of suitable capacity lined with hard rubber, lucite, or bakelite; and for prolonged plating a cooling coil may be necessary to keep plating solutions within reasonable limits of temperature.

CADMIUM PLATING — Cyanide is used almost exclusively in cadmium plating operations. Cadmium plate provides good rust protection and is often used on iron or steel sculpture as a base for brass or bronze deposits.

Solution

cadmium oxide — 3 ounces per gallon

sodium cyanide — 18 ounces per gallon

Conditions

current — 15 to 30 amperes per square foot; 2 to 4 volts

anodes — cadmium bars

The ratio of sodium cyanide to cadmium should be maintained at approximately six-to-one to minimize the rate of sodium carbonate formation and subsequent reduction in cathode efficiency. Periodic additions of sodium cyanide will need to be made to maintain the proper ratio.

BRASS PLATING

Solution

copper cyanide — 4 ounces per gallon

zinc cyanide — 1½ ounces per gallon

sodium cyanide — 7 ounces per gallon

sodium carbonate — 4 ounces per gallon

Conditions

metallic copper — 3 ounces per gallon

metallic zinc — 0.7 ounces per gallon

cyanide — 2.5 ounces per gallon

current — 3 amperes per square foot of cathode; 3 volts

anodes — 80 percent copper, 20 percent zinc bars

room temperature

A few drops of ammonia per gallon of solution will aid in producing a uniform color.

BRONZE PLATING

Solution

copper cyanide — 5 ounces per gallon

zinc cyanide — 0.5 ounces per gallon

sodium cyanide — 5 ounces per gallon

rochelle salts — 2 ounces per gallon

Conditions

metallic copper — 3 ounces per gallon

metallic zinc — 0.2 ounces per gallon

cyanide — 0.3 ounces per gallon

current — 2.5 amperes per square foot of cathode; 3 volts

anodes — 92 percent copper, 8 percent zinc bars

Kenneth Armitage,
Tiger-Tiger, 1966.
Aluminum.

135

Metal Spraying

Metal spraying or metalizing is a process which involves feeding metal in wire form through a specially designed gun. The wire is automatically fed into a flame produced by a burning mixture of oxygen and acetylene. As the tip of the wire melts, a blast of compressed air sheers off molten droplets of metal and projects them onto a surface to form a coating. Almost any metal which can be drawn into wire form can be sprayed with the metalizing gun. Typical materials include brass, bronze, stainless steel, monel, and carbon steels. Sprayed metal coatings range from .002 to over 1 inch, depending upon the material applied. A suitable chemical solvent should be used to clean the surface to be metalized. Porous metals should be preheated to drive out oil or other foreign matter.

Right
Harold Jacobs, *Dog*, 1967. Wood, acrylic putty, sprayed aluminum, 12″ x 36″ x 20″. Photo by Mark Kaltenbach.

Metalizing gun. Courtesy of Metco Inc., Westbury, New York.

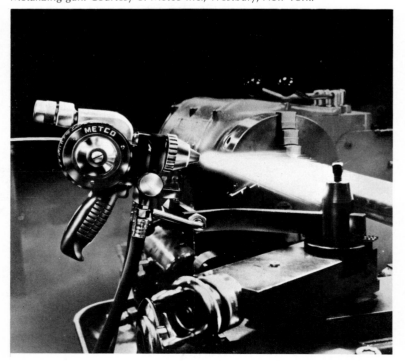

Patination

Patination or chemical coloration of the surfaces of metal is almost always due to chemical corrosion. The most common method oxidizes the sculpture in a bath of chemicals compounded to produce certain colors as corrosion occurs, then, by means of a stop bath or water rinse, the corrosion is arrested at the point where the desired color and surface quality is reached. There are so many variables in the process that it would be extremely difficult to match an existing patina or even develop the same patina at different times.

Methods of applying chemicals to the surface are not unlike cleaning operations. Dip tanks and swabs for the application of cold chemicals are the safest and reduce the risk of over-oxidizing the surface, eating through thin sections of a casting, pitting or otherwise ruining the metal surface. Cold chemicals work slowly, however, and may take days or weeks of application and exposure to produce the desired effect.

One method of developing a patina rapidly is to heat the metal surface with a torch and while it is hot apply the solution by means of dauber or brush. This process can be dangerous to both the work and sculptor — an overheated metal surface may cause the solution to spatter and give off large quantities of toxic fumes. The heated metal surfaces cause the water in solution to evaporate rapidly leaving acid concentrates to act on the metal. Frequent flushing of the surface with cold water is necessary to reduce the concentrates left by rapid evaporation.

BRASS, BRONZE — The following formulas are designed for use with brass or bronze with high copper content (more than 80 percent):

Green   1. ammonia — 5 fluid ounces
sodium chloride — 6 ounces
ammonium chloride — 6 ounces
acetic acid — 1 quart
2. ammonium chloride — 6 ounces
copper sulphate — 1 ounce
water — 1 quart
3. ammonium chloride — 16 ounces
copper acetate — 8 ounces
water — 1 quart

Brown   1. liver of sulfur — 3 ounces
water — 1 gallon
2. ammonia — 4 fluid ounces
potassium sulphide — 1 ounce
barium sulphide — 4 ounces
water — 1 gallon

Black   1. barium sulphide — 1 ounce
ammonium sulphide — 8 ounces
water — 1 gallon
2. ferric nitrate — 8 ounces
water — 1 gallon

Bright black   hydrochloric acid — 1 gallon
white arsenic — 32 ounces
antimony chloride — 20 ounces

water-free; temperature 150° F

Blue   lead acetate — 4 ounces
sodium thiosulfate — 8 ounces
acetic acid — 4 ounces
water — 1 gallon

temperature 180° F

Crystallized surface   copper sulfate — 8 ounces
ammonium chloride — 4 ounces
water — 1 gallon

STEEL

Black   1. caustic soda — 80 ounces per gallon
potassium nitrate — 50 ounces per gallon
temperature boiling
2. sodium thiosulfate — 3 ounces
water — 1 gallon

ALUMINUM

Black   1. caustic soda — 4 ounces
calcium chloride — 1 ounce
water — 1 gallon
temperature boiling
2. potassium permanganate — 10 grams per liter
nitric acid — 4 milligrams per liter
copper nitrate — 25 grams per liter

room temperature

Blue   ferric chloride — 60 ounces per gallon
potassium ferrocyanide — 60 ounces per gallon

temperature 150° F.

Anodizing Aluminum

Anodic oxidation of aluminum produces surface coatings with excellent protective qualities. The oxide coatings are quite unlike the metal itself. They have high resistance to corrosion, and because of their porosity coloring dyes and pigments can be absorbed to produce a wide range of colored surfaces.

Anodizing is an electrochemical process which converts the surface of aluminum to an oxide when the metal is made the *anode* in certain electrolytes. Sulfuric acid anodizing with direct current is the most widely used anodic oxidation process; alternating current may also be used but requires twice the time. Equipment similar to that used in electroplating may be used.

Solution

sulfuric acid — 18 percent

Conditions

cathode — lead sheet approximately the size of anode

current — 12 amperes per square foot of anode; 12 volts per minute

temperature — 70° to 74° F

time — thirty minutes

tank lining — lead; plastic; rubber; ceramic; glass

Colored anodized coatings are produced through the absorption of colored organic dyes and pigments into the pores of the anodic coating. After anodizing, the sculpture is thoroughly rinsed in cold water (hot water will seal the pores and dyes will not be absorbed). The dye bath is prepared in a glass or ceramic container. Concentrates usually vary between 1 and 5 grams per liter of dye. Additions of small amounts of acetic acid are used to provide evenness and intensity.

The following are some dyes and recommended conditions.

Common cloth dyes, Diamond and Tintex, also work exceptionally well in coloring the anodized surface of aluminum. Greatly increased concentrates of the household dyes are necessary; as high as 25 grams per liter may be necessary for adequate coverage. Most dye operations require a thirty-minute immersion period. Longer immersion does not ordinarily produce additional change in color.

DYES FOR ANODIZING ALUMINUM

DYES	CONCEN-TRATION (g./l.)	ACETIC ACID (c.c.)	TEMPER-ATURE (°F.)
Red			
Azorubine extra	5	1	180
Polar red G. conc.	5	1	180
Guinea red	5	1	180
Cloth red 2B extra conc.	3	1	180
Acid orange GC crystals	8	1	180
Erie chrome orange R	5	1	190
Yellow			
Quinoline yellow P	1	1	190
Wool yellow extra	5	1	200
Aluminum yellow A	5	1	200
Blue			
Aluminum blue A	5	none	150
Niagara sky 6B	5	1	190
Black, Brown			
Nigrosine J. crystals	7	1	190
Neutral brown Rx	5	1	190
Green			
Naphthol green B.	5	2	200
Direct erie green Gy.	5	none	200

SETTING — After the dye bath the sculpture may be set in a nickel acetate solution of approximately 5 grams per liter at a temperature of approximately 200 degrees Fahrenheit. Immersion in the setting bath for about fifteen minutes sets the dye and increases water fastness. An additional bath of boiling water for approximately fifteen minutes will further set the dye.

Surface treatments of the aluminum including etching and polishing should be completed prior to anodizing. If polished before anodizing the underlying metal will impart a high metallic sheen to the colored surface.

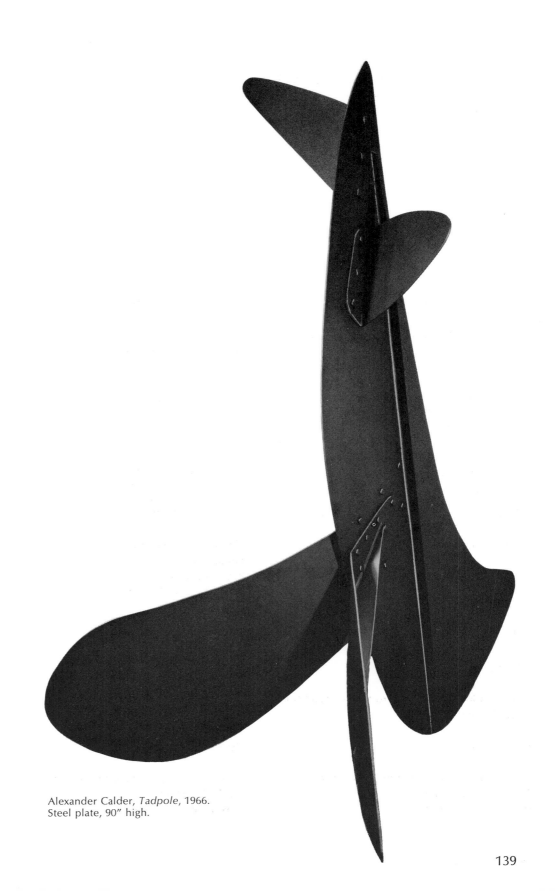

Alexander Calder, *Tadpole*, 1966.
Steel plate, 90" high.

Sources of Supply

CASTING

Alexander Saunders & Co., Inc.
Precision Casting Equipment and Supplies
9 Bedford Street
New York, N. Y. 10014

Bareco Wax Co.
917 Enterprise Building
Tulsa 3, Oklahoma

United States Gypsum Co.
4215 Baltimore Street
Kansas City 11, Missouri

McEnglevan Heat Treating & Manufacturing Co.
P. O. Box 31, 700 Griggs Street
Danville, Illinois

CASTING KILN AND FURNACE

A. D. Alpine, Inc.
11837 Teale Street
Culver City, California

CASTING CRUCIBLES

American Refracturies & Crucible Corporation
North Haven

FINISHING

Metco Flame Spray Equipment and Supplies
1101 Prospect Avenue
Westbury, New York 11590

Metalizing Co. of America, Inc.
3520 W. Carroll Avenue
Chicago, Illinois 60624

Southwest Smelting & Refining Co.
1712 Jackson Street
P. O. Box 2010
Dallas, Texas 75221

WELDING

The Lincoln Electric Co.
Arc Welding Equipment and Electronics
22001 St. Clair Avenue
Cleveland 17, Ohio

Union Carbide Corporation
Linde Division
270 Park Avenue
New York, N. Y. 10017

Airco Co.
150 East 42nd Street
New York, N. Y. 10017

SCULPTURE SUPPLIES

Sculpture House
340 West 42nd Street
New York, N. Y. 10018

Alexander Sculptural Supply House
305 East 31st Street
New York, N. Y. 10016

Bibliography

Albert, Calvin, quoted in Sam Hunter. "New York, Art Capital of the East." *Art in America*, 42:36, December, 1954.

Arnason, H. H. *Modern Sculpture from the Joseph H. Hirshhorn Collection.* New York: The Solomon R. Guggenheim Foundation, 1962.

Arnheim, Rudolph. *Art and Visual Perception.* Berkeley: University of California Press, 1957.

Campbell, Lawrence. "Lassaw Makes a Sculpture." *Art News*, October, 1956.

Chaet, Bernard, *Artists at Work.* Cambridge, Mass.: Webb Books, Inc., 1960.

de Creeft, Jose. "Statement on Sculpture," *7 Arts #2.* New York: Permabooks, Doubleday and Company.

Dewey, John. *Art as Experience.* New York: Minton, Balch & Co., 1934.

E.A.T. News. Experiments in Art and Technology, 2:1, March 18, 1968.

Ferber, Herbert. "The New Sculpture: A Symposium." New York: Museum of Modern Art. An unpublished typescript of the meeting in the Library of the Museum, 1952.

Friedman, B. H. *School of New York: Some Younger Artists.* New York: Grove, Evergreen Books, 1959.

Giachino, J. W.; Weeks, William; and Brune, Elmer. *Welding Skills and Practices*. Chicago: American Technical Society, 1967.

Grohmann, Will. *The Art of Henry Moore*. New York: Harry N. Abrams, Inc., 1960.

Hunter, Sam. *David Smith*. New York: The Museum of Modern Art, 1957.

————. "New York, Art Capital of the East." *Art in America*, 42:36, December, 1954.

Jefferson, T. B., and MacKenzie, L. B., eds. *The Welding Encyclopedia*. New York: McGraw-Hill Publishing Co., Inc., 1951.

Lassaw, Ibram, quoted in Lawrence Campbell, "Lassaw makes a Sculpture." *Art News*, 53:27, March, 1954.

————. "Ibram Lassaw." *Arts*, 1955.

Lippold, Richard. "Variation #7: Full Moon." *Arts and Architecture*, May, 1950.

Lynch, John. *Metal Sculpture*. New York: Studio-Crowell, 1957.

Meilach, Dona and Seiden, Don. *Direct Metal Sculpture*. New York: Crown Publishers, 1966.

Miller, Dorothy C. *Fourteen Americans*. New York: Museum of Modern Art, 1946.

Mills, John W. *The Technique of Casting for Sculpture*. New York: Reinhold Publishing Corp., 1967.

Moholy-Nagy, L. *Vision in Motion*. Chicago: Paul Theobald, 1947.

Mumford, Lewis. *Art and Technics*. New York: Columbia University Press, 1952.

Museum of Modern Art Bulletin. *Painting and Sculpture Acquisitions, January 1, 1961 through December 31, 1961*. New York: Museum of Modern Art, 1962.

Myers, Bernard. *Sculpture: Form and Method*. New York: Reinhold Publishing Corp., 1965.

Nickford, Jaun. "New Talent U.S.A." *Art in America*, 41:45, Winter, 1956.

Oxy-Acetylene Welding Manual. Chicago: Chemetron Corporation, 1950.

Read, Herbert. *The Philosophy of Modern Art*. New York: Meridian Books, 1955.

————. *The Art of Sculpture*. New York: Pantheon Books, 1953.

Ritchie, Andrew. *Sculpture of the Twentieth Century*. New York: Museum of Modern Art, 1957.

Rodman, Selden. *Conversations with Artists*. New York: Capricorn Books, 1961.

Rood, John. *Sculpture with a Torch*. Minneapolis: University of Minnesota, 1963.

Roszak, Theodore. *Fourteen Americans*, ed. Dorothy C. Miller. New York: Museum of Modern Art, 1946.

Sawin, Marticia. "Ibram Lassaw." *Arts*, 30:22, December, 1955.

Seitz, William C. *The Art of Assemblage*. New York: Museum of Modern Art, 1961.

Smith, David. "Sculpture." *Architectural Record*, 88:77-80, October, 1940.

————. "The New Sculpture: A Symposium." New York: Museum of Modern Art. An Unpublished Typescript of the Meeting in the Library of the Museum, 1952.

Struppeck, Jules. *The Creation of Sculpture*. New York: Holt, Rinehart and Winston, 1952.

Tefft, Elden C. "Lost Wax Sculpture Foundry Equipment Sources and Prices." Lawrence, Kansas: 1964. (Mimeographed.)

————. *The Oxy-Acetylene Handbook*. Union Carbide Corp., Linde Division, 1943, 1960.

University of Kansas. "Proceedings of the National Bronze (or Sculpture) Casting Conference, 1960, 1962, 1964, 1966." 4 vols., Lawrence, Kansas: 1960-1966. (Mimeographed.)

Wilenski, R. H. *The Meaning of Modern Sculpture*. London: Faber and Faber Ltd., 1932.

Woldman, Norman E., Ph.D. *Metal Process Engineering*. New York: Reinhold Publishing Corporation, 1948.

Ziegfeld, Ernest. *Art in the College Program of General Education*. New York: Teachers College Bureau of Publications, 1953.

Index